Short Pants No Underwear

By Sarmukh Singh

Singaporean Sarmukh Singh at 56 years old is a Flight Engineer who has nurtured a writing ambition since young. His profession allows him a lot of reading, writing and thinking time, essential ingredients for a writer.

His first book "Short Pants No Underwear" is about life in multi-racial Singapore and Malaysia, ranging from deep personal memories of the various places he had stayed, depending on where his Police Officer father was stationed, to taking satirical swipes at family members' antics at gatherings. He often mixes his descriptions with humorous asides and slapstick.

He is now busy with his second book about his life in the Airlines.

Acknowledgements

Thanks to my Family , without whom there would be less tales to tell and for their courage in giving me permission to use their names in this book.

Also to my good friends, Winston Baptista, A Dass, Michael Leong who have been so supportive.

Victor Tang and Jerry Peacock for their trust.

My children, Sheryl, Desiree , Tasha and Hanz, who were recruited as part-time editors.

My sisters, Banso and Kulli for their faith in my 'writing' abilities.

My dear wife, Jita, who endured my endless hours at the keyboard and thought it was just an excuse for me to have another drink!

And my Mother, Mdm Ranjit for her prayers for my success.

Thanks also to the National Arts Council of Singapore for their backing.

Not to forget the Society of Singapore Writers, (especially Maurice Neo-President), for their encouragement.

Supported by

Author   : Sarmukh Singh

Editor   : Maurice Neo

Illustrator : Sujata Bansal (www.sujatasart.blogspot.com)

Publisher : Sarmukh Singh

Production in Singapore by

Colorcom Graphics Pte Ltd

ISBN 978-981-08-5774-5

Short Pants No Underwear

CONTENTS

CHAPTER 1

PISSA PARTY

As my son, Hanz, lifted himself from the floor of the patio to go to the boys' room, Father, sneaking a quick glance at Mother, hissed a conspiratorial whisper, *"One from the fridge, Hanz"*.

Banking on a woman's total and undivided attention for kids, Father was caught completely unaware by what spouted forth from Mother.

She had been minding her hyper-active grandchildren in the garden. She was as sharp as ever. Normally nothing that concerned the command and control of her household bypassed her, but on this occasion, Father thought she was fully distracted by the kids.

That is why he was unprepared for the verbal outburst from Mother's mouth. It stunned him! She shot across the moonlit lawn, *"What are you asking for? Another beer? The Doctor has ordered you to cut down on booze, and you have had, what, three beers already!"*

Ever alert, her ears acting as mini powerful all-hearing radar receivers, even at a fair distance from the patio, Father's ever so quiet request did not escape her!

Talk about woman's multi-tasking abilities! Mother is a shining example of this, though of the vintage kind.

Their wary grandson stood uncertainly, not knowing what to do, looking helplessly in turn at his grandparents and me, shifting from one leg to the other.

If he fetched the beer, he would receive hell from the Matriarch of the Family. If he did not, his Grandfather would hold it against him and most likely use it to make his life utterly miserable when fancy suited him.

He would be done for in either case.

Life's not so straight forward, fortunately or unfortunately.
It's an intermesh of self-interests.
And mine had reared its ugly head.
I had needed a beer too.

Using the native guile of a kampong strategist, I had thought up a scheme. Knowing how my kith and kin would react when pants are soiled in public, I used the revulsion of that as an excuse to send Hanz to the loo.

A red herring truly! A distraction!

Obviously, what I had really intended was for him to get off his butt to fetch thirst quenchers of the adult kind. But, I, like Father, had not factored in Mother's vigilance.

For my hapless son, it must be said that his Father's wiles had rubbed off on him in great abundance.

He had understood my need without much ado and dutifully rose to fulfill it.

His hidden talent as an actor with a keen eye for improvisations manifested at this point.

With crossed legs, he muttered *"Aiyoh, cannot tahan, cannot tahan,"* (can't hold it any longer), mainly directed at his Granny.

She, like the rest, knew that there was zero tolerance for pants-wetting in this family.

She understood if he had to go, he had to go, but nothing beyond that. (Maternal instincts did not fathom that he had also to fulfill subtle parental demands to replenish the good old beers.)

What was upper most in her mind was that if he did not reach the toilet immediately, his bladder would most probably play him out in front of everybody!

And in this family, one did not pee in one's pants publicly, as memories were long and unkind and the episode would be retold, rehashed and embellished along the way, much to the embarrassment of the guilty party, until kingdom come! (As a couple of bed-wetters had found out to their eternal misery).

Even at his tender age, Hanz knew the culture which his family had lived with all his life and so did his granny.

So, with fake trembling thighs, he looked at me in acute despair, for help.

Well, I had to find a way to let the poor kid off the insidious hook and to make myself look good.

As far as I was concerned he was enroute to emptying his bladder while secretly restocking me with other more palatable liquids.

In the softest of tones, I said, *"Run to the loo, boy."*

By slipping in, while looking at my brothers, *"And on your way back, get us a couple of beers. We need more beers. Right?"* I was trying to rope in my elder brothers for support.

None came, though they would have coyly consumed any beers that happened on the scene.

My son did me proud. He committed the *'perfect'* crime.

With a brilliant alibi installed, he ran straight for the fridge instead of the toilet. He was back with cans clutched in his hands and under his armpits, much faster than the time required for his supposedly desperate pee. With time to spare before his granny got back to the patio, he did another lightning sortie.

Any airline would be proud of his efficient delivery under pressure.

But my 2 siblings - darlings of Mother, could not even force a smile witnessing the great ruse before their eyes performed with such amazing motor skills. At the same time, credit could be given to them for not revealing my intentions. Possibly, they were really in need of a beer too and selfishly, letting me do the dirty work.

They would silently congratulate me if my son and I succeeded and likely be the most vociferous in condemning me if we were caught out.

Always in an ingratiating mode with Mother, they gave me blank stares, as though my beer mission could not possibly interest them.

They had always relished making me the dunce. But they had no chance then due to my son's speedy service. By the time Mother came in from the garden we had already started downing the furtive beers.

But the brotherly pretence still went on nonetheless.

When offered more beers a bit later, Tara, the eldest brother, whimpered *"Me? Oh, I still have half a can left. No worries. I had enough. You go get yourself one if you want."*

The other older brother, Kip, refused to meet my eyes, turning away as though tending to his kids. So with much dutch courage, I had to slink to the kitchen to refresh myself.

Seeing the beers when I returned, Mother glared full moons at me. *"You never change!"* she seemed to shout through her eyes.

Such is my lot. The incorrigible whipping boy.
Always the Fall Guy.

ME, The Patsy who always got blamed for the things I didn't do, or became the centre of attention, whenever, I suspect, there was nothing better to talk about; the spice of gossip to while away the time! Though on this occasion, I do admit, I asked for it. Even though my intentions were for the good of the parched!

We were gathered at my house for the birthday of my pre-teen daughter, Tasha.

The clan present consisted of three generations of our family; grandparents, parents, sons, daughters, grandsons, granddaughters, nephews, nieces, cousins and some of the in-laws.

Sprawled on the patio on a cloudless, moonlit and brilliant star-studded night, after a do-it-yourself pizza party, the adults were supposed to be having only a few beers and reminiscing about old times while the children and grandchildren played in the garden or watched the sky for glittering passing satellites, some of which you could set your clock by, as they always passed over at the same time every night.

I had returned from the kitchen having fetched three beers, one for me and 2 for the Old Man, (one hidden

from Mother's eyes in case he needed another later.)
I settled in a corner on my cushion.

Energized by the surreptitious beers, Tara, without preamble, took centre stage to exclaim: *"Do you all remember the time we were in Bentong when we saw that huge snake stretched across the road? That's the experience I will never forget!"*

His daughter, Nisha, bleated a shrill request at him to tell us about it.

"Oh, while you are doing that, don't forget to tell her about your broken arm," our eldest sister, Beeba, teasingly interjected.

"Or when I nearly drowned!" Banso gustily shouted.

Tara's hogging of the limelight was short-lived.

Being overly sensitive, he was not entirely happy when the indiscretions and boo boos of his younger days were revealed to all and sundry. So when my elder sisters were bent on spilling past beans, Tara lost his appetite to continue.

He judiciously withdrew with a weak wave of his hand, mumbling something about tonsils and passing the buck to me to say something.

With all the children now looking at me expectantly, I had no choice but to comply.

CHAPTER 2

THE BIGGEST SNAKE IN THE WORLD

Quite a few in Singapore, where I now reside, would do anything to stay in our Bentong hilltop house.

By comparison, high-rise flat-living a la public housing in Singapore is akin to being mired in a concrete jungle with few opportunities to mingle with raw nature.

Besides, in my view, the lack of a horizon, being surrounded by tall buildings, and the eyes not having the opportunity or occasion to focus on objects over long distances, has led to a high proportion of children wearing spectacles! And the dependence on computers for studies and games, has not helped at all.

I might be wrong, but just ask the optometrists who are doing a roaring trade!

In Bentong, which is at the foothills of the central mountain range in the state of Pahang, from about 100 metres elevation, we had a panoramic commanding view of the whole town, even as we relished in the silence and isolation amid greenery in our own Shangri-la, that you seldom enjoy in a built-up city state.

To reach the house by car, we had to ascend a narrow winding road with many hairpin turns and z-bends to complete the journey.

The road was lined on both sides by thick bushes and overhanging trees forming a cool, clinging green tunnel almost all the way up.

By foot it was a long steep climb straight up the hill; a nightmare when it rained, since the steps were cut out of the hillside, reinforced with planks of rotting wood - some of which were missing - making it a slippery, sliding dangerous mission!

It was a climb not for the faint-hearted.

It was difficult enough when it was dry. But when laden with a school bag, holding an umbrella during the rainy season, it was an ascent that taxed our fitness. The only use of the folded umbrella was to act as a support while climbing, but even that was impractical, as the tip of the umbrella would sink into the mud and had to be hauled out!

Then it had to be washed when we reached home and put to dry, a tedious task in itself as the clinging mud had to be scraped off every outer rib and covering of the pesky umbrella.

It was easier to leave the umbrella at the bottom of the hill and arrive home wet and muddy, retrieving it the next day or so.

Or simply not take the umbrella to school!

All these huffs and puffs in unpolluted surroundings were not only well worth it; as the destination and hot delicious food prepared by Mother more than made up for the efforts, but the exercise itself in refreshing air was precious and rare, with immense physical benefits. Not surprising then, that all the kids involved did well in school sports! (Yeah, that's what we think on reflection now, but at that time it was an exhaustive experience.)

We often looked forward on rainy days for Mother to pick us from school, but those occasions when she did that were not really that frequent, Father having had to use our Limo, and we mostly had to trudge through the sludge and struggle home.

(I believe the house has been converted to a restaurant at present. Maybe I will visit there one of these days with my family. That would be nice!).

On sunny weekends, we used to slide down the hill in cardboard and wooden contraptions after hosing down the hillside with water to make it nice and slippery.

You bet there were many sore bottoms at the end of the day!

That is how Tara broke his arm.

One day, sliding down uncontrollably, screaming at the top of his voice, ululating in a teenage shrill, and sounding like the hee-hawing of a demented adolescent donkey, he hit the road at the bottom of the hill and catapulted out of the box onto the hard tarred road!

It necessitated a tearful trip to the local hospital to set his broken arm.

However that experience did not deter him at all. The next time the family took out the boxes and the rubber hoses, he was right in front, with his arm in a sling, audaciously demanding his hierarchical turn!

A clout on his rowdy head from Father settled that and he spent the next enjoyable hour (for the rest of us) sulking on the top of the hill! (When I related this to the gathering, it was obvious why Tara balked from narrating earlier, and the kids teased him about it while he was shooting ballistic missiles with his eyes at me).

Well, I had not brought the subject up in the first place!

"What about the drowning?" exclaimed the kids.

Reluctantly I continued. I did not want Tara to be too upset with me. (After all, I was just the messenger, even though I had been hijacked by him to tell the tale.) And he was elder too!

And in my family, we do have respect for our elders. It is inborn or hammered into us right from our weaning days!

Behind our house was a rubber plantation.

Occasionally Father led exploring expeditions through the rubber estate and into the primary jungle that luxuriated on the hills behind our house. He would normally carry his 12-gauge shotgun with him in case of chance meetings with wild boars with their broods or even a cantankerous tiger.

The whole family tagged along, Mother having packed a huge picnic lunch; and a bottle of mosquito repellent and a vial of Chinese medicated oil, which seemed to work better!

One day we discovered a clear stream with many shallow pools. On further uphill ventures, we found a mini waterfall.
This was paradise!

Surrounded by the trees that provided spotted shadows, the water in that stream was cool with small fish and shrimps darting about in the crystal clear water.

That waterfall became our favourite picnic spot for the time we were in Bentong.

Well, all good things come to an end and it was not long before that came by.

It happened when my sister, Banso, almost lost her life in that stream.

We kids sneaked to our spot one day when our parents had gone to Ipoh to attend a wedding and left us in the *good hands* of wily Tara, with strict orders not to get up to mischief while they were away; or else!

And what did Tara do a mere hour after their early morning departure, but to imperiously suggest a hike up to our waterfall and have a swim!

Wow! We cheered and set off after a rapid gathering of our swim paraphernalia and food and such.

It was blissful - the cool stream and the waterfall were fun! We splashed around and jumped in and out of the pool, shouting with the sheer exuberance of it, without any thought of a lurking tiger.

All of a sudden, my sixth sense did not feel right. I looked around and could not see Banso. We searched all around and finally saw a hand frantically thrashing the surface of the pool just below the waterfall. She had slipped and fallen into a deeper part and her foot had caught in the rocks at the bottom. She could not free herself.

Luckily the water was crystal clear and Tara, being the tallest at the time, dove down heroically to release her foot.

She surfaced, frantically gasping for breath, and recovered after some worrisome minutes. The others, especially our esteemed minder of the day, Tara, begged her not to mention it to our parents when they came back from their trip.

But, lah, lah, lah, as in all large families, there is always a big mouth, *(mulut bechok)*, whether intentional or not.

During dinner the next day, when our parents had returned, Kulli inadvertently teased Banso about her spluttering and coughing after she was hauled out of the stream.

My God!

Mother's ears, small that they were, but ever tuned to the special frequency of a dedicated house-maker, loving mother and police officer's wife, pricked up at this.

The inquisition that followed just lacked the bright lights in our eyes and sleep deprivation of the Nazi tortures, but it drew every single detail from each of the guilty parties, that is; all of us.

Of course Tara and Beeba took the brunt of the scolding, being the eldest of the family.

Even though Tara had been the hero and saved Banso from a watery end, he was given a right royal toasting!

His love of the outdoors and ultimately, golf, persists till today. The permanent heavy tan of a *toasted* look that he sports now is always the brunt of jokes. It is supposed to be an indelible mark of the toasting he got from our parents on that day!

After that *drowning* incident, we kids were expressly forbidden to visit our Shangri-La on our own unless our parents accompanied us.

Having a rubber plantation behind the house with primary jungle not too far away meant a lot of visits by snakes and other animals, like wild boars, to our immediate grounds.

Tigers sometimes roared in the distance while whooping monkeys added to the daily chorus.

Father used to hunt the boars occasionally, from which Mother prepared the most delicious curries and barbeques. We have a belief in our family that those who have not tasted Mother's fresh special Bentong wild boar dry curry have not lived their lives yet!

(The fact that when hunting alone at night once, Father had to scramble up a tree after a wounded boar turned on him and planted a tusk in his thigh, is normally not mentioned, so I will not discuss it here. Also that he was alive because the tusk missed his femoral artery by 1 cm. And also that he did not come down from the tree until daylight...........)

"Ok." Nuff said.
Like I mentioned, we respect our elders!

Once, when we were on that winding road leading up to our house, returning from an evening Bollywood movie, the headlights on our Austin A40 picked up a dramatic spectacle.

The road must have been at least 4 meters wide.

Stretched across the road was a huge python. The tail was out of sight in the bushes on the left side of the road. Almost to the edge of the road on the right, the python was stopped in its tracks by a mongoose!

What made it amazing was that the mongoose normally only confronts cobras.

The mongoose is a small animal.

Facing a living, breathing thing; with a mind to kill it or eat it and that is of your own size or smaller than you, is one matter.

But this situation was ridiculous!

This mongoose could not have been more than 3 kilos in weight.

Its intended meal was a minimum of 6 meters of mean, coiling, strong, elastic muscle with a huge toothy mouth at one end. That snake must have weighed at least 50 kilos.

As thick as a grown man's thigh, or my waist at that time, it lay there in the glare of the headlights, flicking its massive pink tongue in and out while the little upstart of a mongoose barred its way, arching it's back , fur standing at ends and body swelling up to appear bigger than it really was.

I mean, really, how big did it think it looked?

It was an extremely fascinating and comical sight. One lunge of that massive snake and it could have swallowed up little mongoosy without even bloodying its teeth!

However the eco-system works in mysterious ways. Natural instincts are super-strong in the animal kingdom and sometimes we don't understand them.

I, for example, outweigh a cockroach thousands of times, yet I scramble for cover when one flup, flups around my head! I am conditioned to fear a cockroach after just one episode with those vile insects.

And what about these two creatures of the wild playing out this macabre road show?

Enemies for untold eons, they must have had mutual respect for each other, size notwithstanding.

Maybe at one period of time the mongoose had been as large as a horse with teeth like daggers!

Memories in the animal kingdom are long and lasting, (or maybe more so in the present human society, but that's a different story, and may be dealt with later too).

We watched this stand-off for at least 3 minutes, the mongoose making a few obligatory passes and the snake hissing and avoiding the puny strikes. They must have realized that they were at an impasse. Neither was hungry or angry or maybe stupid enough to go for the kill.

They looked around and smelt and saw a common enemy.

Humans!

That was our family in the car.

The mongoose slowly deflated, the massive python relaxed its coils, and warily eyeing each other and our car, they slunk off into the bushes on opposite sides of the road.

That was when we realized the actual size of that python. Even when its head stretched full out into the bushes on the right, the tail was not in sight!

Father estimated it was at least 6 meters long.

My parents were worried after that incident.

A python of that size, capable of swallowing a full grown boar, was not conducive to a peaceful state of mind when you have a large family that is used to sitting out or playing in the garden at night or even venturing out in the plantation.

(Visit You-Tube and you can see a python spitting out a Hippo when threatened by hunters! Go on, I dare you! And just a couple of years ago, a full grown Chinese man was found in the belly of such a creature in Taiping, after being swallowed in his own backyard. The python had been killed with machine gun fire by the local police and most probably the unfortunate dead guy in its belly did catch a few bullets too, adding insult to injury!)

However, Father believed that he had an early warning system in place in case of a snake or tiger invasion in our compound.

That was our mighty Dara Singh, a vicious canine, who had a tendency to bite and mutilate anything or anyone within reach of its stinking rotting canines.

(Moreover it was a local belief that a snake would not enter a territory if a dog is around.)

Mother had her doubts though, having seen the massive jaws and size of that python, that Dara Singh could handle it.

There was an occasion when Dara could have been tested, but as usual, he was tied up when the incident happened in the grounds. To give credit to the mutt, it occurred out of his range of vision.
(But he did have a final say in the matter!)

My elder sister, Banso was playing hide and seek with the rest of us and went to hide at the rear of the house where we had unoccupied separate quarters for servants-as they were called in those days. (Nowadays they would be termed as domestics).

She noticed a black shape in the drain that she mistook for a bicycle inner tube. As she was reaching down to pick it up, I happened to 'catch' her. She straightened up and tried to run away from me.

I will never forget that moment.
As if in slow motion, the 'bicycle tube' stiffened and rose up. I yelled a warning.

She thought I was shouting because I had *'found'* her. It is fortunate that she chose this instant to attempt to escape from my clutching hands.

Horrified, I saw the black snake, for that was what it was, lunge at her with hood fully deployed. The vicious dripping fangs narrowly missed her skinny leathery leg!

It was only when she saw the upright cobra that she started screaming, which brought the whole tribe running.

This was a 2 and a half metre long black cobra!

It slithered away and disappeared into a hole beneath the outer wall of the servants' quarters.

Father fired all six shots of his revolver, which was always within his reach, into the hole.

The police were called and they dug into the cavity, which was not very deep.

The cobra was found, shot twice, but still alive.

It was killed, hissing and spitting, with many blows of heavy spades and pieces of hard bamboo and wood wielded by a hoard of sweating, cursing, and frightened policemen.

I had, in the meantime, fetched my hockey stick, but only managed to land a puny blow to its mutilated head after it had been separated from the body by a policeman swinging a parang.

This futile action did make me feel good and brave, though. Macho!

By this time Father had fetched his double barreled shotgun loaded with shot heavy enough to kill a tiger, but it was not needed.

So he put it aside and had a beer to cool down.

That is when Dara Singh dastardly decided that it would contribute to the mayhem. It mangled the hand of one of the policemen who was trying to do the friendlies with it and to stroke its unruly unwashed smelly head. The poor Chinese chap had to be sent to the hospital for treatment!

"That was quite a dog. I never liked the brute. It tried to bite me many times", Mother now said.
Father just glared at her and was silent.

He slyly sucked out the last drops of the warm beer in his can and leaned back against his padded seat.

Though many years had gone by, we all knew that our Old Man had been very attached to that mad, mangy mutt.

Without him making it obvious, we knew that, deep down, he missed that dog, Dara Singh.

"Hey Sam, why don't you tell us about the day you took Dara Singh to school?" Kip suggested.
"After all it was your bright idea!"

"No way was it my idea!" I protested.
"It was the teacher who started it all."

"Please Dad, tell us what happened?" my dearest daughter, Tasha, asked.

I again had no choice but to exercise my vocal cords.

Father was desperately trying to signal that he was thirsty, but I ignored him for the moment.

After all, in the short time I had been talking, he had managed to finish two beers!

FAMILY FIEND

Teaching, like all jobs, can get boring.

But not all teachers make the effort to break the monotony of their lives, much less relieve the grind of school life for their pupils.

My sweet lower primary teacher, Miss Nunis, was however markedly different. She went out of her way to spring surprises on us, making the classroom more like a playground filled with exciting unexpected challenges.

She decided one day on the spur of the moment to go beyond the syllabus by inviting us to bring our pets to school!

I was immediately in a conundrum. I did not have a personal pet. The closest to a pet we had at that time in the family was our Dara Singh, a pariah dog that my father had rescued from the streets and adopted.

This dog was an excellent watchdog. It watched everything and everybody with its mean beady watery yellow eyes. It did not allow anybody to come within sight and sound of our house.

It did not even let the family members to come within biting distance of it!

One would expect a pariah dog rescued from the streets and duly *'doted'* on by the man of the house, namely, Father, to be grateful and be nice to the people around him.

However, it seemed that its birth-right as a tough street dog never left it. Being adopted into a genteel middle class setting seemingly had no effect on it's genealogy and domestication was not part of its agenda.
This dog was just born mean and nasty.

The only reason that it behaved with Father was that Father would take no nonsense from it and did not hesitate to discipline it with a stick or whatever came within reach of his hands, be it a length of bamboo or an old water hose.
That was the only language it understood.

Named after a world-renowned wrestler from India, it was a 35-kilo mass of mean, mangy, mad, growling, bulging ugly muscle, putrefying blackish-brown fur, broken protruding claws and a mouthful of sharp, odorous, greenish-yellow stained teeth.

Once it carved out its territory, where it was chained almost daily, it fought tooth and nail to keep everyone out of its little patch.

Though it might have had a good guard dog record thus far, we did not trust it because it had bitten its Master when Father turned his back on it after giving it a much deserved bath.

(A good bath was something that probably did not flow with the rough and tumble of gutter living. Being 'over-clean' upset the balance of its natural state!)

The popular saying is that a dog's bark can be worse than its bite. In Dara's case it was the reverse. It was natural for it to just bite without giving any barking advance notice. If anyone came close to its slobbering jaws, it just champed down!

I do not know why Father kept this dog. Even when Dara Singh bit him, he merely gave it a thrashing after muzzling it. This hiding did not help very much.

Dara Singh continued to be its usual unlovable self, snarling, frothing and growling, trying to get a piece of meat out of everyone that came within reach of its jaundiced fangs.

Maybe the fact that it was tied up all the time contributed to its mean disposition.

Being unable to sniff at the neighbourhood bitches, whether they were in heat or not, must have driven it crazy. And since it was not spayed, became absolutely stark raving rabid when it's hormones kicked in!

Such deprivations would drive most nuts, including us humans.

On the other hand, if it had been let loose, who knows whether it would have taken out a chunk of anybody's fanny, a risk Father wisely chose not to take.

Well, as I mentioned, our spirited teacher, Miss Nunis took it into her pretty little head that it would be a good idea if the pupils brought their pets to school and introduced them to everybody.

Sure, bringing pets to school was a great exercise for being in tune with the animal kingdom within our reach, besides hopefully encouraging the start of a live-long interest in biology and all that, in a less academic way.

(Moreover, a lot of people had chickens and ducks and goats and such as pets, but generally the relationship was short lived, as most of the pets were edible and destined for the kitchen eventually.)

May seem cruel now, but the economics of those times were such.

Ms Nunis dubbed the lesson: *'Show and Tell'*.

That was all well and good.

Obviously some kids simply didn't have a pet. They honestly said so, somewhat sheepishly.
They were justifiably excused.

I was made of a different mould.
I was not willing to declare that I did not have a pet!

My overriding wish, consciously or unconsciously, was to be liked and accepted by the teacher, being often enough ignored at home except when it was necessary to find a scapegoat...

How could I not be equal to Miss Nunis' call for a contribution to her adventurous jaunt?

My self esteem was now given a chance to be raised in this exercise.

Teacher gave me a way to prove myself as a success for once.

But the closest to a *'pet'* I had was a triple cross between Godzilla and T-Rex and the Devil!

I had my work cut out for me.
My mind began to tick overtime.
The adrenalin was pumping.

I did not even think at that moment of the extreme difficulty and nigh impossibility of dragging a monstrous animal for an audience with the comely Miss Nunis.

I will not even give you any prize for guessing that the *'pet'* of mine weighed far more than I did and I could not even get close to it!

These mind boggling details I did not wish to entertain but instead immediately tried to enlist the help of my senior, Kip…

The idea hit him like a ton of bricks.

He could not hold his composure, nearly falling off the sofa in disbelief and utter shock.
When he recovered, he stammered, spit spraying, *"Are you mad? That loony dog will tear your manhood off!"*

But, aha, even staid Kip was not above being bribed.

Presciently, I had prepared to negotiate a deal.

So out came a choc bar from my pocket.

That did the trick which no amount of persuasion could match. He was sucked into the venture despite some mumblings that the reward was not enough even as he snatched the damned half-melted choc bar no sooner than it appeared.

I knew his weakness to the T.

Even as we approached Dara Singh, it was straining at the limit of its chain, baring its canines and growling at us, pawing at the chewed up muddy grassless ground around it.

We remain rooted there, hesitating for a long time. When so petrified, we just could not think.

Eventually a seemingly easy idea came to mind.

Quite neatly done as far as Father was concerned!

He had taken to wrapping the jaws of the beast with string to prepare it for a bath ever since the mutt chewed up his leg.

But that was the uncompromising master of the house in action.

However, between us two brothers, it was a case of who was to volunteer for the *'dead hero'* role in the drama to come.

It was a very good idea. All we had to do was to tie its mouth shut, copying Father. The problem was which one of us two would or could or dared to attempt that?

As far as Kip was concerned, his skin was worth more than that measly bit of choc. (That's a matter of contention, which might be dealt with later.)

I felt it was going to be even worse than the proverbial mouse trying to tie a bell on a hungry wild cat's neck. Kip tried to lasso Dara Singh with a noose at the end of a long string, being a fan of Kit Carson.

The noose hit its ugly head and slid off.
Dara Singh immediately pounced, clamped its massive jaws on the string and just held on.

Kip tried to pull the string free but the maniac dog just dug its heels and claws in the mucky ground, with only the whites of its eyes showing.

I thought that its teeth might pop out of its jaws!

Then I had a spark of brilliance!

Since we had a long string and Dara Singh was determined not to let go of it, it was easy enough to lead it round and round the post its chain was tied to!

Each round would shorten the chain until the dog was tethered to the pole and couldn't move! The stupid stubborn devilish dog had sealed its own fate.

We did just that and then took our time to truss it up further with the string by going round sixty-six more times, getting quite giddy by the time we finished.

It worked like a charm!

That brute was attached to the post with meters and meters of string and chain. It could barely move its head, though that did not stop it from emitting fierce grunts and muted howls and baring its dirty sharp mandibles.

We cautiously and dangerously slipped a noose around its head and fashioned a muzzle.

Finally we released it from the string and stood back to admire our handiwork.

Dara Singh was a picture of humiliation.
It stood there with its tail drooping between its legs, a murderous look on its ugly mug. It shook its head vigorously and tried to dislodge the crude muzzle with its paws, but to no avail.

It was too good to be true.
We had succeeded well beyond expectations.
(Or so we thought.)

We took the opportunity to tease it, pull its tail and ears and laugh at it.

Believe me, if he had got loose at the time, he would have gone for more than our buttocks with such a vengeance that it would have made front page news for its sheer gory brutality.

When I was ready to go to school, I untied Dara Singh from the post and pulled at its chain.

For a dog that spent a major part of the day trying to free itself from that chain, it reacted very surprisingly!

It refused to budge from its spot. Obviously it thought that I had evil intentions for it.
(Better the known devil of a spot than some unknown fate that seemed to beckon ominously.)

Well, I might have had, but not on that day.

On that momentous day, Dara Singh was going to make me popular at school! Dara was going to raise my profile in school no other feat could match- not even achieving top grades.
(Yeah, he did! But not in the way I had imagined.)

It took all my strength to get Dara Singh to budge.

All the way to school, down the slippery hill, I had to pull that reluctant scruffy mutt, straining and puffing, while it tenaciously clung to the ground with its huge paws and claws.

Yes, gravity did have a part in getting its big mass to the bottom of the hill!

By sheer physical effort, I managed to drag it to school and arrived exhausted and sweaty, but feeling immensely fulfilled.

I had a Pet in School!
I was now prepared to show it to everyone, especially Ms Nunis!

My fellow pupils were puzzled as to why it needed the muzzle.

The sheer sight of my *'pet'* scared the hell out of most of the kids, though a few tried to touch it.

But the muffled snarls, together with the sight of its hackles rising and the massive muscles bunching up at its shoulders stopped them short.

Clearly this was no tame animal by any stretch of imagination.

Kids, more than others, intuitively knew the *"keep clear"* message of the beast: *"Don't touch me! Don't get near me! I will mutilate you! I don't like you! I will kill you! "*

On top of all that, Dara didn't smell of roses either.
More like the *'Swamp Thing'*, actually.

Ms Nunis was pleased to see Dara Singh and scurried over to welcome it.

But her enthusiasm to meet my pet was short-lived. She stopped cold in her tracks as she noticed the sheer devilish glare from yellow eyes filled with hatred and evil. The drool and foam exuding from its muzzle was furthermore not conducive to excite the innocent and sheltered young teacher.

With a few mumbled questions and nervous incoherent comments about Dara she immediately backed away and started talking to another boy about his cute, oh-so-cuddly rabbit!

She was visibly shaken and had quickly diverted her attention to a more pleasant rabbity of a pet.

Still understandably wary, she gave quick backward worried glances at my dog.

Who wouldn't?
During all this time, the dog had been trying to break loose of the crude restraint over its mouth…

Ms Nunis was bending down to look at a pet mouse belonging to one of the girls, when Dara succeeded in dislodging the restrictive muzzle!

At that moment I was distracted by one of my friends and did not notice Dara licking its gnashers and blearily eyeing Ms. Nunis' mass of wobbling cloth-covered bisected flesh.

I did not have time to shout a warning.
Dara did not hesitate. It went straight for Ms. Nunis' fat juicy up-ended round rump!

The only thing that saved her from serious injury was that she moved slightly forward that instant to pick up the mouse. That took most of her posterior beyond the limit of the rusty chain and Dara's slobbering maw.

Its fangs slashed through her dress and one tooth hooked onto her blue panties and tender skin, leaving her bum exposed with a long thin razor-like bloody gash in her flesh.

She must have leapt one and a half meters into the air! She landed back on earth on all fours with a totally bewildered look on her face.

She reached behind her back and her expression turned to one of horror and pain when she realized that her rear-end was laid bare and her fingers covered with blood. She let out a scream that brought other teachers, the school gardener and the canteen hawkers running into our class.

Dara, meanwhile, had turned its attention elsewhere, dragging the screeching, protesting rickety legs of the rusty iron and wood desk it was tied to behind it.

Luckily none of the other kids and teachers were anywhere near it.

It was panic stations. All hell had broken loose.
People scampered about for safety.
One could actually sense palpable fear in the air.

Within a split second I stood alone with my trouble-making *pet*.

Ms. Nunis was rushed to hospital, a teacher in tow, bandages in hand, trying to apply first aid to Ms Nunis' butt on the run and to hide her exposure from the curious canteen workers.

(She recovered in good time and was back in class in a few days, though it was some time before she could sit down without a grimace.

She must have had a pretty strong constitution because Dara's bacteria-filled mouth was the model of unhygienic conditions itself. I believe it contained more poison than the Komodo dragon and the Gila monster combined!)
I was scolded for bringing such a vicious brute to school and ordered by the Principal to take it home immediately.

Kip had by then conveniently disappeared.

He had been watching at a discreet distance and when the turds hit the fan, he ran.

I was left on my own.

How could I get Dara back home?
His muzzle was broken and it looked as if he was prepared to chew through steel.

Thank heavens that the desk was wedged in the door and prevented Dara's exit.
The scene in that school grounds would surely have been bloody otherwise.

I muttered to that astonished Principal that even I could not get close to that vicious, vile, wild dog.

How, he demanded, had I got that beast to school in the first place?

I had no answer to that.
All I really knew was this had been a golden opportunity to give vent to some bravado and to something gung-ho - turning a street dog into a *pet* - vaguely hoping to raise my self esteem against all odds.

Even if I might subsequently lay out the facts of the case, at that moment my mind was just a blur.

I did not know where to begin, as the past three hours had gone by so swiftly.

It had not really registered in my mind that Dara was actually present at school in the first place!
I had also not factored in my plans that I would have to get Dara back home after school, up that steep hill!

And nobody, especially a Principal, let alone my family, would really fathom my desire to have my *pet* in school and my need to win the acclaim of Ms. Nunis!

Father was called.

Foregoing his lunch break he came, of course, in no mood to be civil to anyone, much less Dara. The poor dog was practically kicked into the car.
Its snarls, malodorous and mutinous countenance brooked no favour from Father.

It was a picture of ironical similarity.
The crazy canine varmint in this instance found his match in an even more irate and angry human master.

From beast, the spleen of Father was transferred to his hapless yet adventurous son, who merely wanted to brighten up his teacher's refreshing project.

But all this was water off the duck's back, as far as the adults' understanding my innate desires.

Such was life.
My good intentions meant nothing.
What's more, I knew that I was definitely in for a severe hiding. Fair enough!

The household goings-on were, in those days, somewhat ritualistic as far as crime and punishment issues were concerned.

But what was harder to take was my paranoia that my *'beloved pet'* Dara did enjoy a snide snigger at the proceedings, feeling that they were my just deserts!
This dog was sometimes almost human!
Of greater import to me was the reaction of the school authorities, like my dear nubile teacher.

It figured a lot in my mind even as the bamboo bit into my skinny behind at home.

After all, I was trying to win acceptance from Miss Nunis and not Father.

But to my surprise and relief she did not make a meal of the incident.

Good on her!

It made me feel that in a backhanded way she appreciated my efforts even though my methods were unconventional. Her muted reaction, not saying much about the incident, did calm me but I still harboured a niggling feeling of letting her, and ultimately, myself, down.

All in, I sampled 5 different schools in the states of Malaysia, and had a couple of teachers with similar bright ideas for *'Show and Tell'*!

But I had learnt my lesson.

No more pets to school or volunteering to enliven any class lessons.

It did dampen my innovative spirits, but then again…, being bitten once, in a way, I shied from any more creative animal episodes.

I was reduced to having *'Plenty to Tell'* but *'Nothing to Show'.* And being a pretty non-voluble chap, it soon advanced to *'Nothing to Show and Nothing to Tell'*!

As for Dara, he was discovered missing one day.

Usually such dogs, even pariah ones, returned after being on the lam for a few days, always leaving urinal scent to mark their passage home.

But when Dara broke free he did not return. The possibilities of him suffering fatal injuries cannot be discounted.

Perhaps it had bitten someone who was not so tolerant like my father. Maybe it was knocked down by a vehicle while crossing a road since it was not road-wise, being tied up all the time, as it had probably lost its motor skills.

Or it might have headed the wrong way and gone into the rubber estate and met that gigantic python and lost a test of strength, cunning and evil!

And tigers love dogs as a meal.

Whatever it was that happened to it, we will never know. Suffice to say that normally such a dog does return to the hand that feeds it.

Father did look for it around the neighbourhood for the next couple of weeks.

We knew but did not understand, or maybe we did not have the depth of perception to notice those nuances at our age, the love-hate relationship that went on between the psychotic pariah dog and his tolerant but stern master. Eventually he gave up the search but not the hope of Dara appearing at our doorstep.

A good time gap was afforded Dara before a new dog replaced him.

"I am glad that Fluffy is not like that!" my daughter Desiree exclaimed, cuddling our mewling Shi-Tzu.

I could see her Grandfather look at Fluffy with veiled contempt. I knew what he was thinking – Dara Singh would have made mince-meat out of our whining little Fluffy!

He surreptitiously opened up another can of beer and looked up at the moon.

I did not know how he got hold of that can, since I was busy with Dara Singh's tale.

"Those were fun days weren't they? Remember the times when we used to visit our cousins in Kuala Lumpur? All of us squeezed like sweaty sardines in the car for the whole journey?" Peggy exclaimed.

"Ha, Ha!" laughed Mother. *"Don't leave out the part when you used to throw up all over your brothers and sisters in the back seat!"* I guess she was still upset over those trips when she had to clean up every time Peggy vomited because she was prone to car-sickness, especially on that old winding road to Kuala Lumpur from Johore Bahru.

Yes, Peggy used to get queasy just coming down the hill from our Bentong home in the car! And that was just a trip to school a couple of kilometers away!

Peggy belatedly realized that she had raised a subject that could be potentially embarrassing to her and tried to divert it by calling out to her kids to be careful of the mosquitoes!

It was no use.
The Family had smelled blood and was out to drink it.

Mosquitoes and vampires were nothing compared to us.

(From Bentong, my Father was posted to Kuala Lipis, also in Pahang, and then Johore where we stayed a year in Kulai, and after that relocated to Kota Tinggi. May seem a bit confusing, as far as the story goes, but bear with me.)

Since I already held centre stage, I had to go on.

GROWING UP

Stability is a much mis-used word by people in authority. Be they politicians in office, religious leaders or educators. As a child I was used to frequent chops and changes in my life. In a nutshell, Instability!

My father's career as a Police Officer saw to it that I traveled a great deal not just as a domestic tourist but along with where he was posted in West Malaysia.

Few children can claim to such varied experiences as I have had while I was growing up. I never did understand the modern hype that frequent relocation and change of homes or schools leads to juvenile or psychotic problems in the children involved.

I always looked forward to the next destination and new places to explore and the fresh friends I would make. There was nary a dull year where I had to stomach the boredom of being somewhere too long.

Father had a compulsive tendency to sometimes rouse up the whole family, even on their school days, and set out to different parts of whichever State he was posted to.

In Johore he would take us to places such as the beach at Mersing, or Kuala Sedili in the East Coast, the waterfalls at Kota Tinggi, for a picnic at a strange river,

where at one bank flowed hot water and at the other ran cold water, or up the steep rough narrow road to the top of mysterious Gunong Pulai. Or wherever it took his fancy, whether by car, boat or jeep.
A couple of times even by helicopter!

At Kota Tinggi by the Johore River it was not unusual for me to be roused up before dawn, sat down to a hasty breakfast of hot tea and some eggs and toast while the others were fast asleep.

Most likely it was because my elder brothers, who he used to take along with him on his rounds before, were now in a hostel at the English College at Johore Bahru and the house was infested with females; Mother and my 4 sisters, and the occasional washer woman.

Of course, like some fathers, he had an educational motive on his mind, getting us out to experience something new and connected with his work. The real world, as it was.

And unlike most fathers nowadays, he had the power and clout and interest to carry it out! I certainly had the foundations of an adventurous life which would manifest, much later, in my future job.

As the Malaysians say, I developed a *'Kaki Jalan'* , literally meaning *'traveling feet'* at a very early age! (And I have made the most of it. At the last count, I have visited 87 cities or towns around the world!)

In the pre dawn chill I found myself on a police boat, (fortified against the morning chill by frequent sips of bitter black hot coffee from a thermos flask thoughtfully packed by Mother), that was negotiating the misty, muddy Johore River, to visit remote police outposts that were under Father's charge as District Police Chief.

At these stations I was lorded over like a Little Maharaja by the Police Personnel and the Penghulus (*Headmen*) of the villages we visited.

These were simple folks with hearts of gold.
It was inevitable that a touch of blue-blood aristocratic feeling came over me, though I must not have made it too obvious!

What I mean is that I did not act like a spoilt brat, for I was made welcome wherever I visited!

Even my knobby knees and skeletal frame, which were frequently laughed at by all and sundry in my school and family, were not remarked upon by these sweet villagers.

I often left those outposts laden with watermelons, sugar cane, sweet potatoes, and even fish; deep-water king mackerels, snappers, crabs and sometimes the unwelcome sting ray!

Whatever the humble and honest villagers' livelihoods depended on.
Though Father did draw a line where live baby goats and kampong chicken were offered. I must declare that Father was disturbed by these *'gifts'*, since he had made it a rule that he would not accept such.

But eventually he realized that he had to accept the presents as it was expected of him, mainly due to his predecessors, who, generally, had no compunctions or guilt in taking away cartloads of their offerings. If he did not, he would be taken as being displeased with his visit to them!

As for me, I had no idea about his concerns, and enjoyed the attention paid to me!

Sometimes it was a trip all the way across the Causeway (the one that the Japanese in the last World War had crossed and conquered Singapore so easily), to Singapore's Changi Point.

There we would board a boat for Penggerang, a sleepy sandy seaside village on the south-eastern tip of Malaysia since there was no bridge or roadway across the Johore River for access to the eastern shore of Johore from Kota Tinggi in those days.

We spent the day traveling there, and on the way back home, stopped by Cold Storage at Orchard Road to pick up Father's favourite meats and then again at Woodlands to buy oranges, apples, tins of lychees, household goods and other stuff which were cheaper in Singapore in those days.

Now the situation seems to be reversed, with hordes of Singaporeans rushing across the Causeway for cheap food, provisions and petrol, so much so that the Malaysian Government has set limits on certain goods like rice, cooking oil, sugar and various other items that can be taken back to Singapore!
The present exchange rate Of 2.4 Malaysian Ringgit to 1 Singapore Dollar does make Singaporeans feel affluent when they go to Malaysia!
But that is another story and being a non-political person, will leave it to the policy makers.

Once we even set out for Pulau Aur, a tiny speck of coral island 50 miles beyond Pulau Tioman, which itself is about 50 miles off the East Coast of Malaysia from the town of Mersing. (*Pulau = Island*)

We never made it.
We barely escaped death by drowning when a sudden tropical squall caught us between Tioman and Aur in the South China Sea.

The police cruiser nearly turned turtle, almost swamped by 10 meter high waves and howling winds! Most of the crates of supplies, including those with live chicken, and a wireless set for the outpost at Aur disappeared into the roiling sea, washed away from the open deck.

The two fat milk goats tethered to the aft railing must have gone for their first and last fatal swim for we never saw them again.
We were too crowded in that little cockpit of the police boat; a tiny space with 14 bodies cramped into it, to think of anything else but our survival, much less worry about our material possessions!

Fortunately, a decision was made to double back to Tioman which was nearer. It helped in our survival as the wind and waves were now behind us.
As we rockily docked into the rickety jetty at Tioman, the adults were mumbling thanksgiving prayers in their

respective religions, greatly relieved that no one had come to harm. We had to count our blessings most fervently as the whole family had come along this time.

(Tioman now has an airstrip and International Hotels and Resorts that draw tourists from all over the world.)

For the kids the brush with death had not really registered, being too young to worry and fret about life-threatening dangers of the sea. We were still grappling with the disappointment of not reaching the crystal clear waters of Aur as well as the seasickness that overcame almost all of us, especially Peggy who had to be carried almost comatose off the boat and given re-hydration fluids.

Fortunately for her, F&N Ice Cream Soda was in stock at Tioman! (More on that later.)

It was another 2 days when the sea was deemed calm enough for us to return to Mersing from Tioman. As usual, Father took measures to justify our absence from school despite us not being physically ill.
No lame excuses were given, just a simple phone call. Father convincingly told the school that we were on an educational tour. They were not in a position to question a Police Chief!

A willingness to adapt to new schools and teachers and the ability of all the kids to catch up with their school work must also have helped immeasurably in our being able to cope with the numerous and sometimes, confusing, transitions in our lives.

Or maybe we were just born smart!!
Or too dim-witted to let all the changes affect us!
That's for you, the Reader, to ponder upon.

Nowadays it is very common for entire families to pack up for the school holidays and travel to other countries by air or ship.

If anything, they can be a source of some stress. We have heard of parents needing a second holiday after that 'Family Vacation' to recover from one such trip!

During my time, an overseas break was almost unheard of. It was a great luxury few could afford or even contemplate. The most one could look forward to was visiting relatives in different parts of Malaysia or Singapore.

Holidays, so to speak, were most often spent in our own national backyards.

If anyone did travel overseas by air, as Father did, when he flew to London on a DC 3 to get his Law, and landed at 6 Airports such as Rangoon, Delhi, Cairo, and other exotic cities to refuel enroute, it was a matter of awe and envy for those who could not and the traveler made much delicious mileage about the dangers or pleasures of air travel.

And the adventure would be tossed and turned in their chats for years after, what with the usual snowballed exaggerations, to keep things at the same level of excitement, despite having exhausted factual accounts. Most times the aeronautical details were muddled but who cared! Few really understood the technical matters those days anyway, much less the traveler. And nobody knew what kept an airplane up in the air.

But it gave them so much pleasure exercising their vocal chords glorifying a somewhat elitist indulgence!

The normal way to travel in those days was by bus or train. The lucky families had a car, which was invariably filled to the brim and bulging with voluble humans and their 'barang barang'. (belongings)

The small nuclear family had then not arrived. So to be squeezed like sardines was always expected and endured.

Our contribution to the milling masses, for those years, was an average family of 10. If not for Granny being away in India, we could had easily fielded a full football team and probably won a few games due to our fitness level!

Imagine the 10 of us packed into an Austin A40, traveling from Johore Bahru to KL, with 3 in front and 7 at the back, noisily bickering all the way, – the 6 hours it took to reach KL at a blistering, (according to my Mother), 70 kmh, on a winding, rutted road – with jostling lorries lumbered with timber and goods, and you should get a fair idea of the state we were in when we reached our cousin's house.

All this in a car without any air-conditioning!
Oh yes, did I mention that Peggy did not travel well and was almost always throwing up in the car!

She was given a personal plastic bag eventually, but her aim was very bad and timing unpredictable and a lot of her dubious stomach contents had to be cleaned up by Mother along the way.

The resulting smell, combined with the body odour wafting from Tara's days-long unwashed body and the exhaust fumes from the lorries passing by, circulating in the old car with all 4 windows down, especially when we were caught in a roadwork's jam when the air was static, almost made us pass out.

Of course, when it rained, the windows had to be wound up. That's when they fogged up due to condensation coming from our sweat and breath. Mother was kept busy wiping the inside of the windscreen with an old rag to create a small spot where Father could look out and drive.

It was a recipe for an oven-like situation with us ripe for basting! The smell and heat in that little car then intensified so much that we had visions of being in the Black Hole of Calcutta!

It taught us endurance which, nowadays, parents pay through their noses for kids to go to weekend workshops to supposedly simulate trying conditions to build character and life-skills.

Even if we did bitch, it would probably have resulted in a back handed clout from Father, which was difficult enough since he was driving, but if you got his goat up, he could do it with one hand and still keep on his side of the lane!

However, the journey itself justified the means and the various hassles involved in getting to our end-point.

The town of Ayer Hitam, the household word for a break in the journey, afforded the basics in creature comforts. It was unquestioned that we would stop there to get our bodies stretched, fill our guts and do the necessary ablutions.

If Peggy had barfed by then, - which she invariably did, the mess in the car had to be mopped up. She was given a lot of F&N Ice-Cream Soda to 'settle' her stomach and I dare say it did appear to help. Perhaps, looking back, we should have topped up her tank with good old F&N Ice Cream Soda BEFORE she even got into the car in Johore!

Ask any traveler there then, Ayer Hitam always figured as an essential culinary pleasure stop, before continuing to our northerly or southerly destination.

A one-street cowboy town, the motorists on that busy north-south trunk road were beholden to it for the necessary replenishment of body and spirit to carry on to the next leg of their travels. Occupying such an important role, the food had better be good.

It definitely was!

It drew and could sustain generations of hawkers with passed-down recipes, ensuring the highest standards of quality and taste.

To its credit, Ayer Hitam maintained the welcome of a small town with its warm reception of the salivating visitors. People knew each other well, the regular travelers being on a first name basis with most of the hawkers.

But flies also found the place hospitable. Even with the fans running at full speed, they remained barely a wing's breadth from the food.

"We are family", they seemed to say, *"Let us feed too!"*

The urgently hungry crowd of Mommas, Pappas and Children, together with the cries of the hawkers' assistants shouting orders to cooks at the top of their voices and the various gastronomic smells emanating from the diverse hawker stalls, created a special fraternity feeling few posh restaurants in a city can match.

We felt like soldiers on the march. And history has proven that an army cannot march on empty stomachs. All perspiring diners at Ayer Itam seemed to share that belief. An invisible mutual bond!

We eventually emerged from the eateries, drenched with sweat, but with bloated bellies and smiles on our oily faces. The only daunting task for the rest of our journey was to face a putrid flash flood of half-digested noodles from Peggy's mouth!

Hopefully, fortified with her gassy F&N elixir, she would keep all her recent intakes within her!

(Sadly, the good times for Ayer Hitam came to an end after the North-South Expressway connecting Singapore to Kuala Lumpur was constructed, bypassing the town, sounding its death knell.)

If you visit Air Hitam now, it is simply a sleepy old town. It just cannot support anything more than a few hawkers. Its reason for a bustling existence as a traditional pit-stop has well and truly gone. Nothing can rejuvenate it.

Abandoned by the regular traveler, it is a ghost of its former self, reeking of desolation, decay and degeneration.

Sadly the flies are now not just a trademark of its rural small town feature but have become a symbol of its decline, re-emphasizing the point in triumphant buzzing clouds, signaling their territorial conquest.

(A few Express Buses do divert there to visit a truck-stop, but that's mainly because the bus drivers have a monthly cash payment from the hawkers to bring the passengers there. Believe me, eating in that place is only for those people with cast-iron stomachs! Sorry, Ayer Itam, but that truck-stop does not do justice to your past culinary glory!)

Anyway, to continue , we got on the road again, full of drinks and food. Obviously someone or other had to have to empty their bladders or other body cavities! Even though most of us had visited the odorous toilets at Ayer Hitam.
However, due to our languid pace on the road, Kuala Lumpur was still a few hours away.

For urgent cases on the road, Father just stopped by the side of the trunk road and the afflicted ones hopped into the bushes or jungle and relieved themselves!
In this fashion, we eventually reached our goal.

Our destination was the home of our first cousins. While they lived in less modern conditions, the rustic charms of their surroundings more than made up for it.

As children uncorrupted by materialistic scales of judgment, we, in many ways, naturally appreciated the simplicity of their lives, at least at that stage of our consciousness.

Home to them was no more than a wooden structure with an attap roof infested with rats scuttling, squealing, rustling and rutting throughout the night.

They were people less likely to be upset by minor spills of life. One of their trials was that they were exposed to the inclement weather most of the time.

The attap roof was not at all water proof, and during heavy rain, every kind of utensils from metal buckets to big woks, had to be placed strategically in various parts of the house to catch the drips so that the floor did not turn into mush, as it was just beaten down earth.

My cousins took all this in their stride, as it was. It was home to them and they loved it. Hardy and outdoorish, they were happy and tough kids who could be counted on to cope with trying conditions. But material progress always beckons. No one is immune, I suppose.

As the years went by and their economic situation improved, we saw major changes to their house. The most pressing needs were addressed first, so out went the mud floor and in came a cement replacement.

A zinc roof in place of the attap was next. It brought aesthetical change but resulted in the house being hotter than hell!!

It is not hard to imagine the heat that was radiated oven-like by the metal throughout the abode. Not only that, I suppose the house could be spotted from the moon by the blinding reflection of the sun on the zinc roof!

We took refuge most of the day around the cow-shed which was open sided with the cooling attap overhead. A breeze flowed through, occasionally supplemented by tremendous blasts of flatulence from the cows.

I am sure, if the attap over their heads had been changed to zinc, the overheated cows would have stopped producing their milk in protest!

Our next visit saw an asbestos ceiling added, acting as a heat insulator. It was then possible to sit indoors during the day. Those past few months must have a torture for the family! But they seemed none the worse for it, though a couple of them still looked half-baked!

Brick walls came next, together with electricity which was a really gigantic leap. Having had to make do with oil and hurricane lamps all their lives, our cousins did not hide the impact it made on them. And they were visibly and orally proud and made much of switching lights on and off for a long time. A magic show of sorts!

I leave the scenario to your imagination when they eventually purchased a black and white television. Sadly, the reception being so bad, most of the time they were watching *'snow'* on the screen. But they seemed to enjoy that too!

The toilet remained outdoors until sewerage canals were built for the whole district, years later. Since the house was situated next to a disused tin mine in Sungei Besi, there was a lot of open land around it that was covered with bushes, tall grass with razor-like leafs, small trees with a lot of thorns and a mess of gigantic nasty nettles underfoot.

This was the result of denudation and re-growth of secondary vegetation. We kids used to go out in a group in the morning, each one carrying a bar of soap and a plastic mug to be filled up at a gurgling stream along the way.

We then looked for a well-screened spot in the bushes, and duly pulled down our lower garments. It was a tricky time trying to avoid the clutching thorns and virulent ant hills as we assumed a squatting pose and bombed away.

(Kip was once nipped on his willie by a tiny black ant that must have packed more acidic poison than a full grown tarantula and it was swollen for the next few days. Being naturally shy, after the initial treatment and handling of the tender painful member by his Aunt, he suffered in silence thereafter, but he could not avoid scratching at his privates when they itched. What an agony it must have been for him!)

When the initial convulsive onslaughts were done, we carried out shouted conversations with each other waiting for the next bowel movement to come on. Meanwhile there was surely some occasional puncturing of the air by thunderous roars of pungent gas from Tara! Even in such an open area we couldn't run from his gaseous assaults as nature was still calling us, stuck in that unlikely yoga pose.

Toilet paper was a luxury few families indulged in. We simply bathed our bums with the water from the mugs, and then washed our hands with soap.

Morning ablutions over, we would trek back to the house for a bath. And to drink from the water vat before our morning tea.

Drinking water was supplied in big disused kerosene tins filled weekly from a tanker by a Chinese vendor. And it was stored in a big vat which kept the water cool throughout the day by the simple process of evaporation of the water through the porous clay walls of the vat! For bathing and washing, our cousins had a well next to their house. We used to draw up the water using a rope and bucket, filling up an earthenware tub in a roofless wooden shed next to the well, before we took our bath.

The water was quite clear, except when it did not rain for some time. Then the water level dropped about 12 feet and turned brownish-green with bits of algae and, sometimes with wads of frog eggs afloat.

We had to brush our teeth using that water, but I do not remember being put off at that time. It was all part and parcel of visiting our cousins and what was good for them was good enough for us!

(As they say, *"When in Rome......!"*)

Anyway, today they have strong horse chompers while I have shed a couple. That algae and strings of frog eggs must have been good for teeth!

Oh, did I mention that the well was on lower ground then the cow-shed?

So much for sanitized living.

The well water was cool. On overcast days it did get bad, causing me to shiver. My teeth shook in their beds while I hurried my bath-taking. The first bucketful over the body was the worst.

It was almost as if the system was subject to an electric shock! The whole body stiffened, the muscles went into spasms and the windpipe closed up, making it impossible to draw a desperate breath for some long moments. Goosebumps erupted all over the body and choking noises came forth from the throat, *"Yi, Yihh, Yii"*!

Everything shriveled up and trembled. Yes, even the manly part, which did not look very manly on those cold days, seeming more like a shrunken acorn.

Many a times, I just stood there, picking up courage to pour the first bucketful over myself. Tentative handfuls of water on the chest or back only prolonged the icy ordeal.

However once I got started with the first few bucketfuls, it got better and better. I had to contain myself else I could go on and on. It was pleasantly refreshing and I stepped out of the shed feeling perky and ready for anything that the rest of the day might throw at me!

My cousins used to keep chickens and milk cows, with a few goats. The first evening of our visits was spent chasing the hapless chickens to catch a few for dinner. With a great deal of squawking from the chickens and shouting from everybody, some male chicken were cornered, caught, slaughtered and feathered for the evening meal. No meat could be fresher than that!

Our cousins always caught the cockerels, for to serve a hen to a guest among the Sikh community in those days was a great affront. It was considered such an insult that families had been known not to speak to each other for years if that happened!

(Why that was so is a different story and may be addressed later.)

We also helped to milk the cows, clean their stalls and feed them. But my grip was not strong enough to squirt the milk out of the teat and once was almost kicked senseless by a cow which had probably been annoyed by my feeble efforts.

"What a duffer", the cow must have thought, *"This Idiot can't even squeeze my tits properly!"*

In the evening when the cows came home from their grazing grounds, it was our duty to help pick up the dung the cows left on the grounds, mainly using our hands and a couple of broken spades.

The first time I did that, I was very squeamish, the green-brown, almost liquid, messy mass of cow shit felt so yucky. However, subsequently, I was surprisingly willing to help out with that chore. Moreover I discovered that fresh cow-dung does not smell badly. A little grassy odour but nothing too offensive. It is only when it is left to decompose and ferment for a few hours that it begins to stink. That explained why my cousins picked it up while it was still fresh and steaming!

The dung was left in a pile to dry until it was sold to the ubiquitous middleman, a Chinaman, (Yeah, he for sure knew how to strike a profitable deal, dung or not!), who came around to collect it monthly. He resold it as fertilizer to the farms around the region.

There were also a lot of fruit trees like rambutans and guavas and we used to climb them for their fruits when they were ripe. We had our slips and falls from these trees but nothing serious. Our visits petered out as time went on.

A gruesome mishap among my cousins cast a pall over the entire family situation. One of my cousins was killed when a neighbouring kid knocked her down with a bicycle from behind while she was having a long sharpened bamboo stick in her mouth, using it as a tooth-pick. She fell flat on her face and the stick pierced her throat through her mouth. She died on the way to hospital. The poor girl was only 4 years old.

This incident had a depressing effect on both the families and somehow it affected relations between us.
We were transferred to Penang and my brothers did

an overseas study stint. All these contributed to the decrease in contact between the extended family. We saw our cousins less and less which personally was a big regret to me because my Uncle Kernail was a great guy and always made it a grand occasion for all of us, despite his humble means. And my Aunt was pretty voluble and kept us entertained with a lot of stories. Hats off to both of them!

All this narrating had made me thirsty again.
The children were quiet, probably pondering how it must have felt losing someone close to the family, since they had not had the experience yet.

The adults were lost in their own thoughts, distracted. Taking advantage of the situation, I tried to sneak past Father to fetch a beer for myself.
My Old Man knew me only too well. He had been waiting for me to make just such a move. With a barely perceptible nod and a lifting of his index finger, he managed to command another beer. I slipped him a can when Mother's attention, remarkably, was diverted by one of her grandchildren who was trying to get a reluctant Fluffy on the swing in the front yard.

"Stop that at once! Don't you know what happened to Sam when he was still a baby?" she scolded.

I cringed.

Of course, the many grandchildren, especially my children, and Peggy - relieved that her vomitus was not in the limelight - demanded to know what had happened to Sam; that is me.

Mother began, but was interrupted by an earth shattering scream from Beeba. Beeba jumped up from her spot on the floor and scooted into the house. She had just spotted a lizard on the ceiling near the light above us, and having a morbid, maniacal phobia about lizards, she panicked.

We all laughed at her and tried to persuade her to come back. We finally managed to do that and she returned, fearful eyes popping out from her worried pretty plump face, looking for the lizard, ready for instant flight. In fact, at that moment, her face looked like the lizard she was so scared of.

I was laughing the loudest. Kulli put a stop to my laughter. *"You find that very funny, ah?"* she spouted, *"Mother, when you tell us about his incident on the swing, why don't you include his cockroach experience?"*

I was glad that Mother took over for once.
(I will relate what she said, in my own words.)

EARFUL

I spent the first three years of my life in Ipoh, a mining town in Perak. We lived in a sprawling wooden bungalow, surrounded by about half a dozen mangosteen trees and a few durian trees. There were other fruit trees like guava, rambutans, papaya, chiku and bananas. It was a veritable orchard. Throughout the year we had fresh fruit straight from the home grounds!

There were a couple of memorable experiences for me in that house in Ipoh.

One of those explains my horror of cockroaches, particularly the flying type. Even as I write about them, my skin crawls and a shiver runs down my spine. (Though I have my trusty can of Baygon by my side.)

These beastly, obnoxious creatures can't even fly properly. They just flap around, flupp, flupp, flupp, until they grab a-hold of something with their spiny legs and then they crawl up… or down… your body!

Prior to that incident I had not really paid any attention to these ugly, smelly insects, and just ignored them.

One day, while I was looking for a ball in the storeroom under the staircase, I heard a sudden whirring of wings.

I stepped back out of the storeroom, not concerned.
Three or four cockroaches followed me out. They were
flap-flupping around my head. I brushed two of them
out of my hair.
Suddenly one of them flew into my shirt! The feel of
those spiny legs made even my eyebrows and the hairs
in my nostrils stand on end!
I grabbed at it and felt a sharp pain.

Until then, I did not know that cockroaches could cause
an injury.

As I caught hold of it through my shirt, another filthy
beast landed on my ear.
I tried to brush it off.
The next thing I felt was a creepy crawly sensation in
my ear, accompanied by loud scratchy noises.
That insect had crawled into my ear!

What a nightmare!
I managed to shake out the one in my shirt and as it fell
on the floor I squashed it to a pulpy paste with my bare
foot, all the while crying out for Mother.

She heard me all right, and rushed to my aid.
By this time the cockroach's thorny legs had scratched
the inside of my ear and a tiny trickle of blood was

seeping out.

The cockroach, obviously, had no reverse gear and could not backtrack.

(Have you ever seen a cockroach running backwards?)

It tried to dig further into my ear.

Luckily for me, its body was too big to progress too far. I think if it could, it would have burrowed its way through my head and come out the other side and flip-flupped all the way to China!

Mother tried to get it out at first with her all-purpose hatpin. But the more she poked at its backside, the more it scrambled to get its delicate hind part out of pin-point harm and struggled to get into my brain, (which some people might dispute that I possess). And the louder I yelled.

She tried to pull at its rear end, but part of it broke off in her finger nails, leaving a slippery gooey mass and caused the cockroach to scrape even more frantically. Given enough time, it would have dug an underground train tunnel through my skull.

It was a horrible, horrible, feeling - one that I do not care to experience again. Mother drove me to the hospital where all the doctor did was pour some olive oil into

my ear and the cockroach came sliding out!
He gave me some medication in case of infection and sent me home.

Since then I have a morbid fear of cockroaches, the flying variety giving me the worst shakes. I did not like them before, but this invasion of my ear really did it for me.

Whenever I see one, I do not rest until I have hunted it down, and using broom, newspaper, Baygon or whatever comes to hand, exterminated and annihilated it!

"Yucks!" exclaimed Sheryl. *"Who likes cockroaches?"* She shuddered and looked around her furtively.

Strangely, almost all of my family has an aversion to cockroaches.

Only Beeba is scared of lizards.
Perhaps there was a reason for it?
But we never found out what it was.

And I did not help matters.

Once when she was baking biscuits, I fashioned a rough look-alike lizard out of the left-over dough.

I sneaked it into the oven when she was not looking.

The screams she let out when she opened the oven door to check on the biscuits and saw the baked *'lizard'* would have woken up Rip Van Winkle well ahead of his 20-year slumber!

She threw the whole tray out of the window, biscuits and all, hysterically, burning her hands as a result.

Boy, did I get it from her when she found out the truth and everybody was laughing at her! I swear to this day, I feel my left ear is definitely longer than my right.

She was the one who reminded Mother to continue the tale about me, with Kulli throwing in her two-and-a-half cents worth and still cawing about the swing episode, which was surprising, since she had a major role in it.

Again, I relate.

HIGH AND LOW

When I was 2 years of age, I was on a home-made swing we had in our garden. It was attached by thick ropes to a branch of a mangosteen tree.

With the shade provided by the lush deep green foliage of the tree, it was a pleasure to swing, even on the hottest days when not a single ray of sunshine penetrated to the grassless ground below the tree. The day of the incident, I suddenly felt the swing being grabbed from behind, and I was given a hefty push that sent me soaring high up above the ground.

I enjoyed that pleasant neck-snapping surprise because I knew Kulli had come back from school and that as usual she would play with me for a while before she went in for her lunch.

She swung me higher and higher as I squealed on the downswing with my stomach in my mouth and my butt in the air.

Higher and higher, faster and faster, until my cries of joy turned into desperate screams of fear and I pleaded for her to stop because I could not hold on any longer! She did not listen.
Giggling like a maniac, she kept on pushing me harder and harder until I was almost horizontal on the upswing.

Finally, I lost my death grip on the ropes that held the swing!

Wham! I landed on the ground on my face!
I was in coma for three days.

When I regained consciousness, I found my lips were split and swollen and that two of my front teeth were missing. Fortunately they were milk teeth and I did not suffer permanent damage.

My nose was the size of an Ubi Keledek (*local sweet potato*). It was broken and has been slightly crooked since then. I had two black eyes.
And I had been turned to a *'sucker'* because I could only use a straw to feed myself.

No doubt, my sister did get her *'punishment'*, but that was no joy for me as I lost big.

She never dared to give me a push on the swing again!

"That explains your bent nose. How do you explain the rest of your ugly face?" Kulli asked.

She was certainly not pulling her punches!

I started to retaliate, but Mother cut me short by continuing her story.

UP THE TREE

A strange event happened when I was just about 3 years old in that majestic house in Ipoh.

It was my parent's habit to take a walk after dinner, to, as they say in our part of the world, *"Let the food settle"*. While the rest of my siblings were doing their homework, my parents strolled around the extensive grounds.

One clear moonlit night, after dinner, even though I was bathed, powdered, and in my pajamas ready for bed, my parents decided to take me along with them during their romantic walk.
They occasionally did that and I enjoyed being with them alone. It was always a pleasant surprise for me and I looked forward to an invite every time.

I romped around the driveway, skipping and running all over, chasing my own shadow and a few fireflies that were darting around.

At night the garden looked very different than it did during the day.

It was almost mysterious but I had no fears at all. I was born and bred in that house.

Even the refusal of my elder brothers and sisters to sleep in one of the rooms did not bother me.
After all, I slept where they slept and there were plenty of rooms in that house to choose from!

According to Mother, during that walk I stopped at a frangipani tree to take a pee. Suddenly I stiffened, screamed and fell down! I did not wake up until 2 days later. (I seem to have been doing that a lot, don't I?)

Father took me to the hospital in Ipoh where the doctors could not find anything wrong with me, all my bodily functions being normal. I was just unconscious, that's all! It appeared as if I was in a profound sleep.

My parents spent a deeply worried two days until I suddenly snapped out of my slumber. The first words I uttered were, *"Nenek (old woman or grandmother) want coconut!"*

Though not really superstitious, my parents were not unbelievers of the *'other world'*. They realized that my problem was beyond a normal doctor's scope. Something out of the ordinary did happen in my case!

They had paid little attention to their children's complaints that the middle bedroom was unpleasant to sleep in. Now they put two and two together and decided to take some action.

Through his contacts, Father arranged for a *'Bomoh'* - a local medicine man and witch doctor who dealt with the occult - to pay a visit to our home.

This gentleman, a wizened old Malay, dressed in a faded beige long-sleeved shirt, checked blue and green sarong, with a tattered black songkok on his head, came to the house the day after I was discharged.

It was explained to him what had transpired the night I lost consciousness and the demand from a *'Nenek'* for a coconut. He was led to the frangipani tree where he visibly recoiled.

Muttering prayers under his breath, he was next shown the suspect room. Prayer beads and a Koran in one hand, coconut in the other, he did not enter the room immediately.
He seemed to converse with someone inside the room and proceeded to enter with visible reluctance.

Mother, who was standing next to him at that time, told me later that she felt goose bumps and the hairs at the back of her neck stood on ends!

The Bomoh motioned Mother and me away, entered the room and closed the door behind him.
All the time he was chanting prayers from the Koran.

We heard grunts and groans from the room. The Bomoh shouted a few times at the top of his voice. We could not understand the language he was speaking. At first his murmuring was soft and continuous. Then, his voice reached a fever pitch and he was almost shrieking. Sometimes, he read out verses from the Koran.

Once he shouted, *"BIS! BIS! BIS!"* very loudly, making us fearful for him. He also shouted, *"Go away! Take your coconut! Go in peace!"* a few times.
There were sounds of a chair being thrown across the room and other objects crashing about. We were worried for him but dared not look into the room.

After about 45 minutes he opened the door. He looked tired and pale. He was sweating profusely and his whole body twitched and trembled. His *'songkok'* (sort of a cap worn by muslim gentlemen) was askew on his small head.

I fetched a glass of water which he gulped down gratefully. When he recovered his composure, he smiled weakly and in a shaky voice, told us, *"Sudah pergi"*. (It's gone).

Mother led him to the living room where he collapsed on the sofa, babbling to himself and clutching the Koran to his forehead.

When he opened his eyes again, he narrated to us what had transpired in that room. Before he entered the bedroom, he had tried to communicate with whatever was inside and heard susurrations while he requested permission to enter, out of respect for whatever entity resided there. The moment he closed the door to the room, he heard a fierce whisper telling him to leave or to face harm to himself.

Apparently the resident ghost sensed that he was a threat to it. He said that he had seldom faced such an evil presence as in that room.

The croaking voice belonged to an old woman whose family had been squatting on the land before the house had been built.

When the developer got the contract from the government to develop the land, he had managed to chase out or pay off all the squatters except this feisty old dame. The toothless old crone refused to move. She was forcibly evicted from her squalid hut and it was torn down in front of her tearful eyes.

In the process of struggling to prevent this from happening, she rushed towards the hut and was run down by a tractor and crushed to death. In her dying breath, she gasped out a curse at the developer.

Her spirit took up abode in the room when the house was built since that was the spot where she died. She did not normally disturb the occupants as long as there was no perceived threat from them.

However, my brothers and sisters did feel her static malevolent presence and that made them uncomfortable and unwilling to sleep there.

In the evenings she liked to sit among the blooms of the Frangipani tree. (A tree usually associated by Malaysians with the dead and whose flowers are used in wreaths, for reasons not clear to me.)

She had been doing that for a long time, minding her own business, lying dormant and doing nobody any real harm.

Then I had to come along!

The sight of me peeing on her favorite tree was too much! I had desecrated her resting place.

She exposed herself to me in her most hideous form and I screamed and fainted.

The Bomoh said that though she had been passive for so long, she had to be got rid of now because she had, for the first time, actually shown herself to a living person. From now on, getting bolder and stronger , she would seek to inflict harm more often. She had tasted meat, so to speak.

He had a hard time getting rid of her.
She was a very stubborn old biddy.

I can imagine the difficult time the developer must have had with her, and have often wondered whether he was still alive! Or if he was dead, how he died.

The chair was flung at the Bomoh, together with other loose objects in the room. It was only his experience and knowledge of the black arts and his belief in his Koran that saved the Bomoh and enabled him to banish her from the house and its grounds.

Though he assured my family that it was safe to use that room, none of us dared to venture into it after that, even during the day!

My parents also ceased to take their romantic after-dinner stroll henceforth.

The haunting tale set my niece's tongue wagging again. Having heard 2 incidents of my being rendered unconscious she justifiably deducted that I had spent quite a fair part of my childhood comatose.

"Wow! This uncle of mine has not been conscious for much of his life, has he?" Sharon commented.

The hush of the audience was of a particularly unsettling sort as it had been a long while since we as a family had gathered to recount such spooky stories.

Their huddle was tighter than usual as they were given a true life account rather than picking up such tales from the TV.

I could sense that at anytime someone would go berserk with fright and scream at the slightest noise. Even Fluffy, in my daughter's arms was wide eyed, taking in the fear radiating from its mistress.

Father took the opportunity to sneak away while everyone was engrossed in the Ghost of Ipoh, and Mother was having a sip of her iced rose water.

My 'incident' prone nature was not let off lightly.

Peggy went on: "You think that it was the last time that that had happened to him? Let him tell you a couple more experiences we have had trying to keep him alive. Though I really do not know why we bothered!"

"Hey!" I protested. "Why is it always me the baddie. You can't really blame me for all those problems. Many of them were caused by others who were supposed to look after me!"

"Shut up! Get on with it" Peggy ordered me.

She was elder then me, and respectfully, though reluctantly, I took a sip from my can and continued.

Shortly after that ghostly experience, my Father was transferred out of Ipoh. We went to Bentong, a small town in the hills close to Cameron Highlands, where we had met the python.

SPIDER HUNT

On the move again.

Barely into the second year, our nomadic ways caught up with us and we parted with such sweet sorrow from our short love affair with Bentong, the birth place of the Malayan Communist leader Chin Peng.

The next hop was to Kuala Lipis within the same state of Pahang. We seemed to be shuttled from one communist hotbed to another. It must have been Father's good record in dealing with the communist insurgents.

I was too young to understand that and I never even thought about the political goings on in my country. My business as far as I was concerned was to enjoy myself, so long as I went to school and did my education, as my parents desired.

Eventually after less than a year in Kuala Lipis, we ended up in yet another security risk area, Kulai in the Southern state of Johore. After that it was Kota Tinggi.

The ups and downs of life still went on, even as the itinerants got going.

There are moments we all face that make us feel, rightly or wrongly, that the end is nigh, no matter where we are.

These could be sickness, accidents or family problems.

Lots of kids look forward to the occasional flu or fever so that they could stay at home for a few days as long as it does not develop into a full blown disease.

The extra attention lavished on them by members of the family especially by the Mother is most welcome!

(But the catch is how to be only a little sick - just enough to escape school, but not to see it so prolonged and worsened that you suffer too much to enjoy it.)

Once in Kota Tinggi, I contracted typhoid. My temperature reached 41.5 deg C. Medics would probably confirm that that is on the dangerously high side with grave immediate complications like brain damage.

Emergency home cure came fast.

When I started convulsing in the middle of the night, my parents quickly filled the bathtub with water, dunked some ice cubes into it and immersed me naked in that cold, cold water! I must have passed out for I have only a vague recollection of how it felt.

Thanks God for being the 7th kid in the family.
My parents had long years of practice in providing first aid in such circumstances.

Submitting a kid with high fever to this kind of treatment still goes on, I believe, at home or in hospitals.

I am told my eyes had already begun rolling in their sockets and I was having severe spasms.

There was no way I could have lasted the 10-minute drive to the hospital without the quick icy action of my parents!

As soon as my temperature came down slightly, they drove me to the hospital where I was warded and diagnosed as having typhoid.

I was in hospital for a good 10 days. The fever fluctuated wildly. My hair fell out in clumps and my mouth filled with painful sores. I ached all over. Even my eye sockets had the most excruciating pain for a couple of days. My anus was almost inverted, and bleeding.

I sweated and suffered for almost a week, which passed in a blur of thermometers and wet towels, injections and watery faeces.

When the worse was over I rather liked the recovery period. I was pampered to a degree I was not used to. Recuperation over a few days was quite pleasant.

My family was at my beck and call.
Anything I wanted was provided for me.

I seldom had so much attention paid to me by Father and my brothers and sisters! I regarded myself as the ugly duckling of the family and quite resented, maybe rightly so, and maybe subconsciously, the way Mother seemed to favour one of my elder brothers over the rest of the family.

I realize now, being a Parent myself, that it is inevitable in any multi-sibling family for parents to favour one particular child over the rest of the children, however much the parents may try to avoid this situation.

Sometimes the mother may have a different favourite son or daughter than the father's. This is the most serious situation as it can lead to problems between the parents themselves!

Whatsoever, that stay in hospital made me realize that even though my parents seemed to pay an unequal attention to their children, they actually loved all of us and would do anything to protect us from harm.

It also showed me that my brothers and sisters really cared for me.

When I returned home and entered our house on wobbly legs after my stay in the hospital, I was profoundly touched and surprised because my family had put up a big welcome-home banner in the living room!

There were also flowers in the bedroom for me!

But the honeymoon period had to end.

I felt really down when I was fully recovered a few days later and had to revert to my role as the regular family punch bag!

The other time when my parents were highly worried about me was when I was again admitted to the Kota Tinggi hospital at age 8, for the removal of a pus-filled swollen polyp in my armpit. I was supposed to be warded for only two days in the hospital after the surgery. It turned out to be a long, long stay of nearly two and a half weeks!

The night before I was supposed to be discharged, I was given wrong medication by the ward nurse.

In those days it was not a normal practice in small town hospitals to test a patient for allergy to a particular drug. Actually, it was up to the attending doctor.

It was only when the patient started sweating and swelling up, turning blue, black or purple or bursting out in rashes and gasping for breath, that an allergy was recognized and efforts were made to keep the patient alive. Most times they succeeded, but unfortunately, some patients did not recover.

In my case, it was already known that I had an allergy to sulphur-based medication due to my earlier stays in hospitals and having had reactions to the drugs.

I was lucky because Mother was with me when the nurse administered an overdose of a drug which had a sulphur content.

Within minutes, my fingernails started turning blue, my face puffed up so that my eyes were hardly visible, and I started to fight for my breath. My legs bent up at the knees and my arms stood straight out from my body!

Mother realized that there was something wrong with me and ran out of the room looking for the nurse.

Luckily, the doctor was on his rounds at that moment and he came running to me with Mother scurrying close behind him, followed by the frantic nurse.

One look at me, and he went to work.

He managed to stabilize me quickly.
He was very angry with the ward nurse and she left my room crying after he blasted her about her incompetence.

From Mother's point of view, it was preferable for the nurse to be in tears rather than Mother being in tears!

Of course when Father arrived from his office, it was the doctor's turn to face his wrath and he was deeply apologetic.

Such are the laws of the human jungle.

The matter did not end there. The next day, the director of the hospital and other senior staff came to visit me and were all sugar and candy.

Boy!
Did I enjoy all the attention paid to me by those doctors and nurses after that episode!
I felt, this time, truly like a little Emperor!

The only downside of that was that the director presented me with a plastic bunny!

What was he thinking of?
What would a full blooded rumpuncious boy want to do with a plastic bunny?

The fact that Father was the Chief of Police in that town definitely contributed to all that tender loving care!
I was in that hospital for a further 4 days before the swelling subsided completely and my fingernails returned a normal pink tone.

I was about to be discharged and did not really look forward to that.
(Little brats, especially those not used to be spoilt, get used to special treatment very fast and do not want it to end.)

Fate however saw it differently.
The morning I was supposed to be discharged, the nurse, a different one then the sulphur nurse, took my temperature-a normal procedure before discharge.

I was found to be shivering and running a fever.
The doctor was summoned and he arrived, huffing and puffing, in record time.

After a lengthy inspection of my sweaty body, and blood samples analyzed, the doctor shakily advised Mother to leave me in the hospital for further observation.

My poor Mother!
This must have been really too much for her. She had already been shuttling between home and the hospital for the past 6 days.

She only had outside help from a washer woman who merely did our laundry.

Mother bore the brunt of all household chores, down to rustling up the daily meals for a horde of hungry youngsters.

That was the most demanding part.
Having a large family did not help. She had to juggle the needs of her other children, before and after school, as well as in this instance, visit me in the hospital at least twice a day.

I was diagnosed as having malaria.
By this time, I was down to the last ounce of my reserves. The shivering, chills and fever took a lot out of my already thin frame.

I remember that that my watery stools were like clay, black in colour and smelling strongly of medicine!
Hard to flush away stool sticking to the bowl!

It was nearly 10 days later when I was deemed fit to be sent home on wobbly, trembling sticks of legs with blurry eyes and hanging folds of skin.
(Not to say that I had any to spare, anyway.)
I am sure that the doctors and nurses were glad to see me go!
They must have thrown a surgical-alcohol drunken party and danced the night away after I left.

But the worst has yet to be told. And this event occurred in Kulai.

At age 6, I shook my parents badly, in an incident that was easily the closest to death I came.

(With my reputation as a hyper active boy it would be been plausible if I had bitten a snake.
In any case, if I had really managed to do such an impossible action, there would have been ready fingers pointing at me for my *silly* deed, and the snake put on a pedestal.)

In our Kulai base I was actually bitten by a banded Malaysian Krait, one of the deadliest local snakes around.

The house that we were staying in at that time was located within the compound of the police station.

Rich with flowering bushes, shrubs and lily plants, our garden was perfect for hunting spiders, which I used to do quite often.

I caught the spiders in a matchbox lined with leaves and coddled them to school where we kids would indulge in spider fights during recess or before school commenced.

We would spit on them, and somehow that got them in a fighting mood, and they would attack their opponents with their fore-legs raised like miniature crabs.
(It could have been our bad breath that got them that way!)

One day I went to the garden in my search for spiders. There was a clump of white lily that was my usual hunting ground, the long green leaves of the lily being favoured by the spiders to make their homes between two leaves by gluing them together with their silk.

I must have been there for only a short while when Mother called me to have my lunch before I left for school. I went into the kitchen to wash my hands.

Mother gave me a once-over to see if I was presentable for school. She noticed a thin blue-black line just above the inside of my right ankle. She bent down for a closer look and her face went pale.

A snake had bitten me, no doubt! The tiny fang marks were unmistakable.
Even as she looked at them, the entry points were swelling up and appeared like miniature volcanoes with bluish-black blood trickling down to my foot.

I had not felt anything until now. But when she returned from locating Father, I was already sweating and feeling slightly dizzy. My leg was also starting to hurt.

Father was unable to come immediately, being away in Johore Bahru to attend a court case. Instead he summoned a driver from the police station in Kulai to take me to the clinic, even though Mother could drive. (She was one of the first Sikh women in Malaya to be granted a driving licence, by the way!)

In this instance, Father realized that serious driving skills were needed, especially when he did not know the type of snake.

This Police driver, a Malay, is one of many who contributed to saving my life. Without hesitation, he lifted me into the car, with Mother holding me in the back seat and engine racing, sped out of the police compound and swung into the main road to Johore Bahru, towards the General Hospital.

Now, this stretch of road was one of the busiest roads in Malaysia, as I have mentioned before.
Being the trunk road from Kuala Lumpur to Singapore, it was choked with all kinds of vehicles, from cars to heavy goods lorries, buses and massive timber transports.

On a normal day it could take up to an hour to cover that distance of only 35 kilometers! That Policeman took just about twenty hectic minutes to reach the hospital in Johore Bahru.

I was rushed to the Emergency room.

The Doctor was at a loss what to do, because he had no idea what kind of snake it was that had bit me. That was important so that he could administer the proper anti-serum.

By this time, I was not in my senses. I had difficulty breathing, my saliva drooling out of my mouth, and my tongue lolling about.

As he was considering his next move, there was a

commotion at the doorway and two policemen came rushing in, holding a big glass jar. Inside the glass jar was the terrible snake!

Realizing that identification of the snake would help the doctors, they had hunted for the vile reptile among the lilies and found it in a very short time. Having killed it, they rushed at breakneck speed to the hospital.

Looking back, if these two policemen had not done what they did, I would have been a goner.

The snake was only a meter long, black with yellow stripes. I was given the anti-venom, preventing further harm from the snake's poison.

I regained consciousness much later.
My leg had swelled up and it was extremely painful.
Other than that I felt quite giddy.

I got a shock though, when I reached for a glass of water on the side table. The jar containing the coiled snake in a bath of preservative, was staring in my face! Somebody had left it there unintentionally, having forgotten to dispose of it!

Well, Mother was very glad to see me recover so fast.

She told me later on that when I passed out in the car on the way to the hospital, she thought that I was going to die.

The Policeman had done the right thing by rushing me straight away to the hospital at Johore Bahru.
We later found out that the government clinic at Kulai did not carry the anti-venom. If he had proceeded there, valuable time would have been lost.

He knew his job. According to the doctor those few minutes were vital to my survival. In fact the policemen who killed the snake had first proceeded to the clinic in Kulai, and not finding us there, had driven at hyper-speed to Johore Bahru.

I still wonder how they did the journey in so short a time! Perhaps, the siren blaring from their police car had helped.

There was a curious outcome to this snake bite saga.

For quite a few years after that, at exactly the same month that I had been bitten, my skin, where the fangs had gone in, would scale and peel off for about a week - a big round patch of scaly, white, dry skin! Even today, you can still see the two pin points where the fangs sank into my bony ankle.

I was never scared of snakes, either before or after that incident. In fact I used to catch snakes without feeling squeamish or frightened.

In Bentong and Kota Tinggi, during heavy rains, when the low lying areas around our house were flooded, snakes would come inside our home because their dens were flooded and that was the driest spot around! It was not unusual to find a coiled instrument of death on the stairs or in our rooms, so we were extra careful during the monsoon season.

The longest snake I caught was a 2 meter black cobra.

It is very easy to catch a snake. All you need is a long bamboo pole with a running noose at the end.

The cobra is a very obliging fellow. When it gets cornered or angry, it raises up its head, opens its hood, hisses, and glares at you.

It is at this point that most humans panic.

Instead, all you have to do is slip the noose over this co-operative head and yank on the end of the string that you are holding. The noose will tighten and the snake will be firmly attached to the other end of the pole!

Then you can take your time to kill it.

I admit that this method works for snakes that are not too big.
I, for one, don't think I would challenge a 6 meter python, like the one in Bentong, with this flimsy contraption.

I would run away!

Surviving the snake bite sure did give me lots of street credibility among the kids. They looked at me in awe.

Most of them had just suffered the usual chicken pox or fever. Few of them had ever had a stay in a hospital.

"Wow!" said my son, *"You are a real Champion!"*

I felt 3 meters tall, for once liking being the centre of attention. There was a rush to examine the snake bite marks on my leg!
My self esteem rose a notch.

This did not last long, because Father came back to the patio, smiling to himself and weaving slightly as he folded back into his seat.

"You did not take any more beer did you?" Mother demanded.

He just shook his head sheepishly and closed his eyes.

I suspect he must have had a quick beer in the kitchen while the tale was being told. Moreover I noticed a strange bulge in his sarong. My suspicions were justified when he shifted slightly to move the cold beer can from his privates! I did wonder how he was going to drink without his wife noticing.

At that point, my little nephew, Sher, came up to his momma and said that he wanted to go to the toilet. She started to unzip him prior to leading him inside.

"Be careful with that zip! Sam had a very frightful experience once!" Kip barked from his corner.
He started laughing loudly and the other older folks followed as they remembered that sorry episode which I would deeply have liked to forget.

It was difficult evading the kids' interest in my mishaps, reluctant as I was to share them with all present.

I just had to oblige.

SHORTS PANTS
NO UNDERWEAR

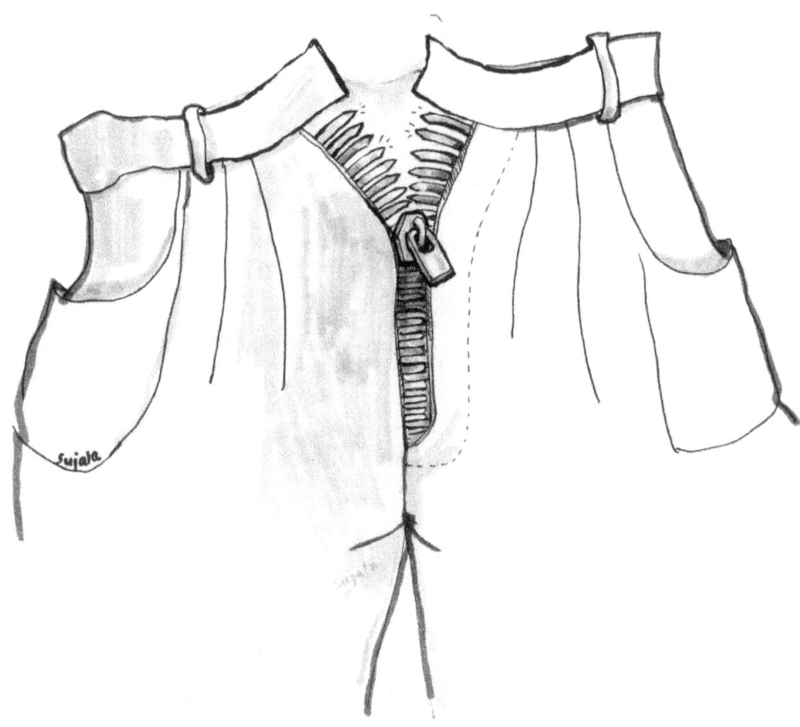

When was the first time you ever wore underwear?

It seems such a strange question in this day and age, doesn't it? Well, believe me, it wouldn't be so odd in my earlier days.

Though the girls throughout my primary school days always had something on under their skirts, (don't ask me how I knew that), I daresay that there were some of us boys who had their privates dangling in the breeze that often violated that airy space in our over-large short pants!

May I say, there was lots of ballroom?

And what a pair of short pants!

Father always believed that his children should grow into their clothes. He was a man ahead of his time. He bought clothes for us 2 sizes too big; at least for the first kid in line.
Besides giving ample room for fast growth at that age, the clothes were recycled. It just made economic sense.

We had no qualms about losing out on the fashion of the day, if there was any that we were aware of! Most of the time we were totally uninterested in, or ignorant of, new styles- even if they existed.

We accepted what was given to us unlike picky present day kids with none or fewer siblings, and the parents just wanting to keep up with their competitive, materialistic and mindless counterparts.

Hand-me-downs were part and parcel of family connectivity. We did feel proud to wear our elders' old clothes. Maybe there was an innate sense that some form of tradition was being passed down.
Besides, somehow, there was the realization that resources were limited. Sharing was inevitable. Siblings were aplenty and everyone had to be fed, clothed, and educated to a reasonable standard.

The shorts I was wearing at that time to school were the ones that Kip used to wear. He was a few years older than me. The moment he grew out of his shorts, they were carefully washed, folded, mothballed and kept in storage for me.
I think they were actually Tara's pants, faithfully preserved for Kip and then, handed down to me, when I was old enough to inherit them. The fact that they did not fit me at all did not enter the equation.

(Fortune smiled on my younger brother, Bally, who was 9 years younger than me. Pass-me-downs were less practical in his case. My shorts (or rather Tara's) either got misplaced or simply were too worn out for use. In any case the times had changed and he was dressed more modern than we ever were!)

My shorts in my first year of school were voluminous! One can say that they were the forerunner of the Bermuda shorts.
But the present Bermudas are sleek and fashionable. Not so during my days!

As I said, my pants were hand-me-downs.

2 to 3 sizes too large for me, they reached down to my knobby knees.
Made of khaki-like material, the washer-woman used to starch them stiff; not with the soft starch we have nowadays, but the no-nonsense rigid tapioca starch. So stiff, that after ironing, the shorts when placed upright on the floor could stand up by themselves!

Can you imagine me putting them on, each leg of that short pants standing out like a wide mini-skirt, with my chop-stick legs inside?

They did not even flutter in the wind!

But they would have made good sails. Should there

been a high wind I stood in danger of being carried aloft all the way to Bombay.

With little material possessions to call my own, I was proud of those pants! They became me!

When I buttoned them up each morning, with the breeze blowing up my thighs, cooling the family jewels, Boy! Did I feel good!!

And unlike some other kids, I was always eager to go to school, except when it came to some lessons with certain teachers whom I did not like because I perceived that they did not care for me.

Anyway I was not really alone in wearing outsized pants to school; there were a few other kids in quite the same boat! Though from my reckoning, mine were the widest of them all.

And those pants were worn with no underwear!
When I sat down, the pants' legs would balloon up, upper edges sharp as a knife, exposing even my crotch. No one batted an eyelid. We were never self-conscious about this.

Because, on rainy days, in our neighbourhood, the kids could be seen running around naked in the rain. Our natural playground consisted of muddy pools, flooded drains and slippery slopes during the rainy seasons.

We horsed around, splishing and splashing. Despite the dangers, some even took to waddling and swimming in swollen drains and swift flowing canals. News of kids drowning was common.

But it did not stop anyone from living dangerously as we were of a different age where braving the elements made up for the lack of artificially constructed toys, cable TV and computer games.

We were completely transparent in our nudity.
There were no secrets between us.

For the first three years the shorts came with buttons. Since most of them were handed down to me, by the time I wore them, the buttonholes had already over-expanded due to wear and tear.

The buttons had an irritating habit of slipping out from the holes, further exposing my Little One to all and sundry!

Not that it mattered to me, but as expected, a couple of unenlightened teachers did notice my exposure and were not too polite in warning me of punitive action if I continued to expose my delicates to the public. I was improperly attired, to say the least.

I told my Parents about the matter, though how I actually brought up the subject eludes my memory.
How do you tell your parents, "Hey, my teacher says she can see my willie when I sit down"?

And that was when it came into my life, the new age miracle, The Zipper!

I was introduced to the zipper at the start of my primary 4 year. What a marvel it was! Just like a new toy.
Being so close to my life-force enhanced its significance.

I would zip it up, zip it down, then zzzippp it up again. Zzip! Zzip! Zzipp!! I felt like a gunfighter.

Zip down, release my water gun and shoot. Then zip it up. Even walking to school, I unzipped my pants, took out my weapon and urinated on the roadside. All for the pleasure of playing with that zip.

Alas, no one had briefed me on the perils of playing with a zip… especially when no underwear is worn…
So, there I was, this bright sunny morning, ambling through the dozens of trees in the Rambutan plantation, a route that I normally used as a short-cut to school.

A sudden urge to play with my zip seized me.

ZZZZzip!!

With one violent motion, I unzipped my pants with my right hand.

With my left hand, I withdrew my Willie, aimed it at the base of a tree and let loose.

Bang! Bang! My enemy lay dead in a watery grave, killed by the vicious stream of liquid bullets blazing from my trusty water machine gun.

My masculinity boosted, I cockily gave my weapon a good shake and tenderly slid it back into my short pants.

Zzip! Up, I drew the Zipper.

And I screamed!

Oh, the pain! The shock!
I was rooted to the spot.
My precious Willie was captured by the Zipper!

I could neither straighten up nor bend down further. Each slight movement brought excruciating pain and agony from my crotch. I couldn't even look down at the zip to see clearly how the vicious teeth had bitten into my lengthy soul!

I started sobbing.
(What else could a young kid do?)
So there I was, crouched in the middle of the rambutan plantation, with my Willie caught in the jaws of a metal monster, tears streaming down my face, unable to move, one hand holding my shorts up, the other desperately holding on to the zip, trying to prevent further mutilation and ultimately, I thought, decapitation.

I cautiously looked around, but there was nobody there.

Home was a half-mile away. There was no way I could make it back to my house in that condition.

I must have stooped atremble there for a full 6 and a half minutes. My knees were shaking, and I was sweating buckets. Finally I realized that I had to do something despite the pain to escape from my predicament.

I plucked up courage, took a firm grip on the zip and gingerly pulled downwards.

Owooo!!!
I yelled out loud and long.

I almost collapsed with the fresh daggers of nauseous pain that hit me. When I looked at my hand, I saw some blood on my fingers. It was terrifying! I thought I was going to lose my dear Willie!

(Had I known at that time that my Willie was just not for peeing, but could be used for a lot more better and pleasurable purposes, I would have, maybe, passed out).

All kinds of fatalistic thoughts went through my mind.

Suddenly, I heard someone shouting.
It was the owner of the plantation.

He was the last person I wanted to meet.

I had a habit of helping myself at times to the fat juicy sweet red rambutans that hung down bountifully from the branches in bunches like huge hairy red grapes and temptingly within my reach.

He used to holler at me whenever he saw me and I would run like hell to escape his clutches. He was surprised that this time I did not move. He ran up to me and angrily demanded what I was doing there.
I did not need to say anything. One look at my posture and my tear-streaked face told him that I was in some bother.

He peered at my shorts, took a glance at my bloodied zipper and shook his greasy hairless shiny head.

I had done a really bad job of it.
The skin was caught in the hungry hooks and was bleeding profusely. He knelt down before me and tried to help.
His touch was enough to make me yowl in agony , only louder this time.

If anybody had come upon us at that moment, it would have seemed extremely suspicious - an old, bald, Chinese man kneeling before a young skinny brown kid, at pants-level, with the kid shrieking his nuts off!

Luckily for him, there was no one to witness this sorry spectacle.

He finally fetched a large pruning scissors from one of his sheds and carefully cut out the front of my shorts with the zip still tenaciously attached to my poor swollen Willie.

He then carried me back to his hut and called Mother who arrived shortly afterwards. She took me to the family doctor who had to give me a pain-killing injection before he cut up that zip with a pair of steel cutters.

Oh yes, those zips in that days were made of steel. They were made to last and to munch up little boys' dicks. There was no more cowboy action from me after that.

I treated that ZIP with a lot of respect!

Though zips did take a little nip now and then at my water pipe, it was never as serious as that first time! I had learnt my lesson well not to treat it as just a toy. I respected it as a vicious flesh munching monster, if given half a chance.

As zips became more common in our school, it was a regular scenario for a teacher to be seen rushing to the toilet in aid of a hapless child who was bellowing his head off and crying for his mother and father and grandparents to help save his mangled precious thingy.

My parents realized it was safer to get me a pair of underwear and that is how I became the proud possessor of three sets of Crocodile underwear; even though for the first few weeks I was always scratching and adjusting my tonnage because I was not used to the constraints of my underwear!

Yes, this was the first item of clothing that really fitted me!

I honestly do not know what happened to my underwear after I finally grew out of them. The elastic had by then loosened and frayed so much that I had to tie knots in it to hold them up.

Like I said, Bally only appeared on the scene 9 years later and thankfully for him, that underwear must have been so moth-eaten that it was not usable anymore. He had to be bought new ones!

I was quite embarrassed by this story, as all the kids were bellowing their guts out; my children and all their cousins, everyone imagining how I looked like when I was stuck in the middle of the rambutan plantation, with my bloodied Willie stuck in the mighty Zipper!

"Boy!" exclaimed my son finally, after regaining his breath. *"Papa that must have really hurt!"*

"Yye...essss," I hissed.

At this moment, Bally, who had been relatively silent up till now, said, *"I bet it was not as painful as the slap he got from his teacher!"* I glowered at him and growled, *"Shut up, you young pup, you were not even born when that happened!"*

The conversation now turned from little *'koteks'* (willies) to learned *'Che'Gu's' (Teachers)*.

"Remember the teacher you had, who used to pass out in class, Kip?" I asked him.

"And Desiree, how about your Malay language teacher?" I directed at my daughter, desperately trying to divert attention from myself.

However, there was no way I could brush this aside. With all the kids clamouring to know what happened with my teacher, I cleared my throat and continued.

And it was a tough night on my vocal cords!

SLAP ABOUT

Mr D. Chen was our P.E. teacher. He was strongly built, of average height, broad about the chest and very loud in the mouth.

To us in Primary 3, he was a veritable Hercules. With his foghorn of a voice and aggressive personality, he had our absolute obedience and attention.

(But he had, in due course, to pay dearly for his indiscretions as a young educator. He was too inexperienced to realize the effect his actions could have in the future.

And that there's such a thing as creating one's own bad karma. Of course, such retribution by the Gods does not happen often to those who most deserve it!

Just look at Idi Amin of Uganda, responsible for umpteen deaths, but he still died peacefully in his room at a Hotel in Saudi Arabia.

......And I have slept in the room too! But that is another story.)

No one would, could, or dared, to challenge or disobey Mr Chen. He especially disliked Indians and was very offensively voluble about it. He never did call me by my name.

The derogatory *'Bai'* he shouted out when he called me was not enough. He had to rub salt into the insult with labeling me a *'dog'* too.

In full flow and at his meanest he would shout, *"Ehh, You! Bai Dog! Go and bring the balls from the store room!"* Or something in that vein.

(*'Bai'* actually means *'Brother'* in our Sikh Language. However, it can also be used insultingly by other races in our region, often targeting the young Sikhs. Of course, they would think twice before insulting a brawny older Sikh gentleman with turban and bristling moustache and a faceful of unruly hairy beard, who would likely tear their tongues from their mouths! There is a reason for the insult but it would take a whole chapter to relate it, so I will leave it to next time. It all depends on the manner it is said and the intention of the speaker. And there is a difference in calling a Sikh a *'Bai'* or a *'Bhai'.* Call a Sikh a *'Bhai'*, and he is your Brother forever! Just don't pronounce it wrongly, or you will have the Sikh on your back for eternity.
And believe me, you would not like a Sikh to get on your back at any time! But more of that later.) Maybe.

But as innocent kids we had already been through a slew of abrasive adults and his racial slurs were just something that we adapted to and accepted as part and parcel of our young lives.
It was no big deal.

In those days, we took verbal, and often, physical, abuse in our stride stoically. Such harsh ill treatment we had to make accommodations for. (This will be reiterated often in some chapters here, so bear with me). We almost expected it and such was the culture that we had no choice but to accept it.

It was part and parcel of our upbringing; not to question our elders or superiors. We went along with many injustices as though they never happened.

However, Mr. Chen did come close to the limits of our tolerance. His physical excesses involved punching, twisting arms and throwing the unfortunate victims to the ground, whenever they fouled up during his sessions. (This was an almost standard behaviour of abusive teachers, as will be seen later, only that Mr Chen did it more roughly.)

One day he gave us an instruction for our PE. I was facing away and did not catch it. Mechanically, I imitated the boy next to me in whatever he was doing.

The next thing I knew was Mr. Chen bellowing and striding towards me with a furious expression on his ugly flat mug. He seized me by the neck, swung me around and roared in my face, his spit splattering all over.

Suddenly, *"Whack!"* My head exploded with stars and I fell down.

That big macho man had slapped me with all his bull strength!

I lay on the grass stunned, my ear ringing and my jaw aching. It took me a long time to recover.
My jaw was painful for 2 weeks after that.

I could not and did not dare tell on him to my parents; even though they noticed the swelling on my face and that I had difficulty eating. I was very scared of my teacher. I just mumbled that I had knocked into the goalpost during a game of football.

Mr. Chen continued his persecution of Indians though he did not slap me again. He did jounce me up and down by my ears, (as if they were not big enough!) and slam my back with his fist from time to time, until the end of that school year.

Thankfully, he was not to teach me again.

And I was not to see him till years later, when I began my working life after post-secondary school, settled in my profession.

As fate would have it, he had joined the same company that I worked for.

I was now his senior. Not only that, I had grown much taller than him, and bigger too!

Looking at him then, I was surprised that he could have terrorized us in school. In a role reversal situation he looked so insignificant and small!

(But on second thought, it doesn't take much to intimidate children, does it?)

When he was introduced to me as my trainee, I recognized him at once.

How could I ever forget him?
He, on the other hand, did not recall who I was.

He was respectful and subservient.
If I did not know, through bitter experience, his violent and racialist tendencies, I might well have been taken in by his false charm.

He was all, *"Yes Sir, No Sir!"*
If I had asked him to get me 3 bags of wool, he would probably have sheared the lamb right in front of me!

Probably his armpits too, if I so desired.

It was only on the 3rd occasion when he came into my office that I put his ugly past before him when I asked him in a quiet voice whether he remembered a small *'Bai Dog'* in his PE class years ago.

You should have seen his face!

As much as it was unpleasant and not something I wanted to confront, I did, I confess, deep down, savour that moment of hubris.

I thought he was going to have a heart attack.

He mumbled an apology, saying something like, *"We were all young then."*

Well, I did not pursue the matter further and left him to fetch some paperwork, his mouth opening and closing, taking deep breaths, gasping like a guppy out of water, eyes agog.

I have not seen him since then.
He probably thought the better of it and just disappeared from my life, forsaking his employment in that company.

Being a bully himself, he must have thought that everybody was like him and that I would have made his life miserable! And being a coward at heart, he could not bear to think what revenge I had in store for him.

As for me it was not as straight forward as he might have thought.

The fact is, I did mull over the matter at home. It just showed how concerned I was about how I should handle the situation in the most professional manner. But his not turning up saved me the headache of a potent dilemma for me and my conscience.
He did both of us a favour by running away!

What a relief!
As I have found out throughout my life, bullies are basically unstable people. If they can get their way with you on one occasion, then God help you.
Expect more trouble coming your way!

Bullies come in all shapes, sizes and ages. If you stand up to them, they run with their tails between their legs.

Before I continue with the rest of my family's memoirs, let me tell you why I am particularly averse to bullies.
I will include it here while the subject is fresh.

BULLY BOY

There are bullies and there are bullies.
Some work on the mental make up of their victims, and these are the most dangerous.

Others are more common and they are generally into physical abuse, but if prolonged, can lead to the victim's mind being affected.

They nestle in respectable comfort everywhere, in our neighbourhoods, workplaces, even in governments and sadly, in our immediate families too.

These predators work on the diffident and vulnerable. They are quick to exploit any signs of weakness in their victims to offset their own shortcomings and insecurities. With such a mindset, bullies know how to select their victims, sensing who to pounce on.

When in Primary 2, I was very happy with my friends. A lot of them had been with me for the past year. My best friend was a guy called Andrew Foo. We used to hang out during our free time in school such as recess time. In class we sat at the same desk and helped each other out with the school work. We paired up during PE and other activities.

Andrew was taller and stronger than I.

We complemented each other - I was skinny and of average height, but more interested in academic work and he more adept at physical activities. We were drawn to each other the previous year and remained best friends in our present class.

All this changed over the next few months and our relationship deteriorated until we split up as a team forever.

The reason for this break up was another boy, or should I say, A Beast, who came into our young lives for a short period of time but affected me profoundly for years afterwards, even until today.

But looking back, I think it was good for it to happen so early in my life. I had had an invaluable firsthand experience which taught me how to stand up for myself and to recognize a potential bully and put him or her (yes females can be bullies too!) down.

At the end of the school assembly one morning, Andrew Foo and I were climbing the staircase back to our class when I happened to step on the shoe of the boy ahead of me. All I remember is that he looked back at me and yelled out.

I stammered an apology.

This boy, Maurice D.V., turned around, poked me hard in the chest and spewed an expletive.

I was caught by surprise and again said I was sorry. He continued up the stairs but kept turning back and staring at me. Not wanting any trouble, I lowered my head and quietly went to my class. Andrew, next to me, never said a word.

Now, Maurice was slightly taller and heavier than me and was in primary 3. He had big bullfrog orbs and ugly, uneven, broad, broken, yellow teeth. At that moment when he poked his dirty fingernail in my chest and I did not retaliate, he must have realized, with a natural born bully's instincts, that he had found somebody he could rely on to take his abuse!

As for myself, I never thought of myself as a potential target. I was a boy who had no enemies, having a reasonably protected comfortable life, not having had many problems with my classmates and teachers.

Life was easy, and one day just flowed into another, with few pressures than to finish my homework on time and produce the requisite results in school.

And to heap on striving to be liked by all and sundry. And to keep a smile on my precious Momma's face when I handed her my Report Card.

(I was used to be picked on occasionally, but it was nothing I couldn't handle, maybe because I had a thick skin!)

Moreover, I had a good friend who clicked with me and I had no need to go out of my way to cultivate new friendships.

In fact, I promptly forgot about the incident with Maurice on the staircase by the end of the next period, though I did have nasal flashbacks of his stinking breath.

Not so, Maurice. No, he did not forget.

How he must have plotted and planned to make my life a misery! How he must have rubbed his hands with glee as he imagined me cringing under his stare. How his twisted mind must have worked overtime to come up with all kinds of strategies to humiliate me! How he must have exercised his thumbs to make them stronger so that he could pin me down under them and grind my soul to mush!

What he came up with was nothing spectacular, when I think about it now.

At that time however, I was terrified and totally in his power, almost mesmerized whenever he confronted me. My knees shook, my mouth went dry and my body became clammy with sweat.

A week after I had stepped on his shoe, I was again walking up the stairs with Andrew when I felt a sharp pain at the back of my shoulder. I turned back and there was Maurice, froggy eyes a-bulging, with a maniacal smirk on his black face.

This time the fear hit me badly. I actually trembled. He didn't say anything, just grinned terribly, reached out slowly and pinched me in the same spot.
I couldn't move.

Then he blew his fetid sewer exhaust of his lungs on my face, stepped around me and jauntily continued up the stairs.

Andrew had witnessed the whole episode.
Yet he did not do anything except to push me forward up the stairs. He never mentioned the incident the rest of the day. Nor did I.

I was ashamed and puzzled by my cowardly reaction to Maurice.

Maurice must have jumped for joy that day!
He had confirmed that I was the perfect victim.

From that day on, Maurice appeared at any time to confront me. I was pinched, punched, pushed, prodded pummeled and punished.

He accosted me as I came in the gates of the school, ambushed me during recess, and tripped me up in the toilet. He even demanded my recess money a few times, which I meekly handed over, going hungry for the day.

Most of the time, Andrew Foo was present. Though I was incapable of retaliating against Maurice, I did not understand the indifference of my best friend. Whenever Maurice shoved me around, Foo just stood to one side and let him carry on.

I began to wonder if Foo was a bigger coward than I was. He was much bigger than Maurice and just a shout from him would have sent that bully sprawling or running for his life.

Due to that reason, as Maurice's attacks escalated, I drew further and further away from Andrew. I no longer waited for him at the school gate in the morning.

Instead, I ran to my class to avoid attracting the attention of that smelly devil.

I started to bring sandwiches to school for my recess and eat them in class. My mother was surprised when I asked her for the sandwiches, knowing my liking for the canteen food, but I told her that I had to catch up with my work and that I had to stay back in class to complete it.

She must have thought that I was a very responsible boy! But the fact was that my school work had begun to deteriorate.

I could not help but to draw further away from Andrew Foo. He, on his part, as I said, never tried to intervene and help me whenever the bully confronted me.

I realize now that, big as he was, Andrew must have been scared of Maurice himself! He was probably embarrassed about this and no doubt petrified that the same fate would befall him.

Naturally our relationship took a dip. I was left unsure of my best friend's character. We might still be polite friends but sadly, the feeling of trust and a sense of camaraderie had been eroded.

On my part I could no longer share my work with Andrew. We drifted further apart .

Maurice continued to harass me at every opportunity. Besides verbal heckling he also continued to manhandle me. I have Maurice to thank for my fluency in the 4-letter word at a very young age!

I became moody and irritable, both in school and at home. My sister noticed this and one day, when I used a filthy word and kicked the neighbour's cat, she took me aside and asked me whether I had a problem.

What could I say?
I was already disgusted with my situation and myself. Many a times I did not want to go to school.
Terrified, I did not even want to step into the school compound. The extortions and attacks on me mounted. I was near paralysis. Depression had almost set in.
The tipping point was near.

But somehow I maintained some reserve of energy and resilience in me or else at any time I could have a breakdown.

I soldiered on!

One day, about 4 months after Maurice started picking on me; I was descending the stairs when I felt a strong push from behind. I knew, without turning around, that my nemesis was at it again.

Without a thought, I whipped around, and blindly threw a punch!

What a punch! What a moment!

The great bully for once got back his own medicine. (Probably the last time too! The Mohammed Ali K.O. roundhouse from me was totally unexpected by him.)

Blood bubbling from his stinking open mouth, eyes almost popping out of his skull, he staggered back before tripping to the bottom of the stairs.

Even as he fell, I jumped down like the Hulk and gave him a kick in the ribs, a bit stunned by my own aggression. But while I could not contain the exhilaration within me, there lurked a forbidding sense of what I had spontaneously done.

I was pumped up and ready to tackle anything, as well as to run for my life!

As Maurice staggered to his feet, I pushed him to the ground again.

I stood over him, huffing and puffing, in a mixture of fright and wonderment that I was capable of such violence, even if in self-defence!

Maurice did not get up again. He lay there, holding his chest where I had kicked him and looked away from my glare.

I just spat on him and stomped off.

That was when I noticed Andrew, my failed friend.

The world loves a winner, I suppose.
He was no different. He had seen the whole incident.

From being a cowardly spectator, he moved towards me, possibly to acknowledge my moment of triumph, wanting to be associated with it.
Or relieved that he did not have to reveal his spineless nature if Maurice had focused on him too.

But in my confused state of mind then, I just wanted to run away as fast and as far as I could from there!
I dragged myself home that day on very rubbery legs.
The prospect of having to face the consequences of my instinctive and quite foolish action haunted me.

On the one hand, I was elated with what I had done and on the other, I was fearful that on recovery, Maurice would catch up with me and break every bone in my body!

What would the next day in school have in store for me?

In extreme trepidation, my anal sphincter in convulsive knots, I went to school the next morning.
True enough, Maurice was waiting for me just inside the school gates.

I could not retreat as he had seen me, and it would be futile for me to try to outrun him.
So, I bravely scuttled on.

Believe you me, Maurice was actually beaming as he approached me, but his gapped toothy smile was something that I had learned to fear.
I thought I was going to die!

Well, I had to keep putting up an act!
I did not want to appear amiable as I could not afford to misjudge his motives.

I stood my ground, staring at him aggressively - ready to defend myself to the death.

Letting my school bag drop to the ground, I stiffened my skeletal posture, a la Mike Tyson.
Without much ado, Maurice reached down, picked it up and started off towards the assembly area.

Can you imagine my shock?
I did not know what to make of it.

In a daze, I stood next to him for the next 10 blurry minutes, but at the end of assembly, Maurice just moved off with a lazy wave of his hand and went to his class.

From that day onwards, Maurice followed me around like a faithful puppy. In fact, in time, we became friends, though I was always wary about him, having seen the darker side of his personality.
I definitely did not seek him out for company!

Is it so, that all that bullies like Maurice need, is a strong punch in the mouth to cure them of their ills?
Must victims be led to the corner with their backs against the wall before they stage a fightback, like I did, whether intentional or not?
(Remember the old story about the mouse deer and the hunting dogs of Parameswara in Malacca?)

In this sorry affair Andrew came the worst off.

Whereas I attained speedy maturity.
To me, he looked a wimp despite being the biggest and fittest of the three of us.

What's more, Andrew lost all the regard I had for him. On being promoted to primary 3, I seated myself as far away from him as possible.

This episode with Maurice had a profound effect on me. I became more self-confident and self-reliant. Subsequently, when I left school and started working, I was able to fend off other would-be bullies and assert myself when required.

If I had not thrown that right hand at Maurice, I feel deep in my bones that my self-esteem would have been affected negatively for life.
I am now so much stronger for it.

"Wah!" said Hanz, *"You must have been the original Karate Kid."*

Desiree was by now all fired up to tell us about her teacher and I paved the way for her to do so, affording her the centre stage.
(Please remember that Desiree is my daughter and her story is set in Singapore, where she was born.)

CHAPTER 12

SHROUDED THREAT

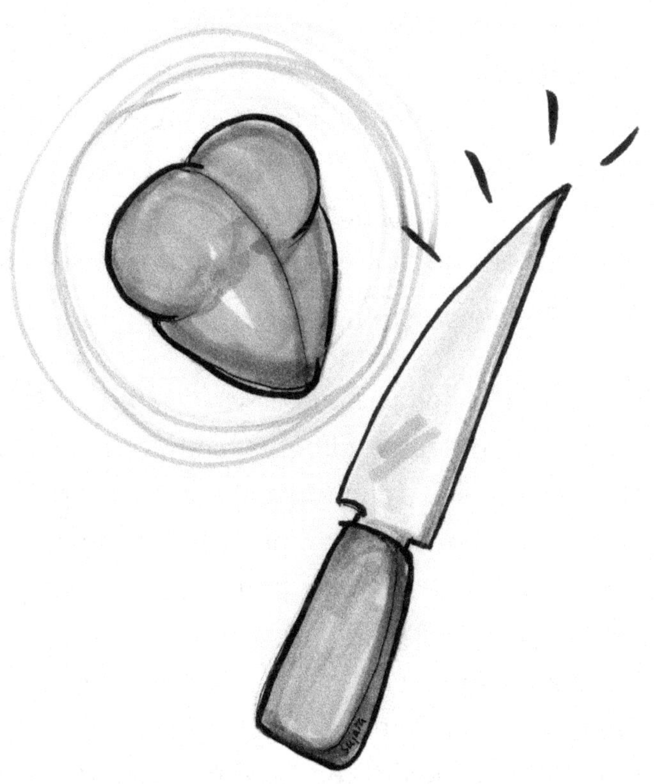

The teacher as the stimulator and motivator of a young child is much under-rated. A teacher, for instance, can make or break a child's interest in a particular subject, especially if the child is slow and ignored or reviled publicly in front of the classmates.

In my view, teachers quickly grow impatient with a student that lags behind in a class, whether it is in day-to-day studies or whether it concerns an assigned homework that is not completed in time. A lot of jaded teachers become either lazy or complacent, maybe due to the day-in, day-out routine, year after year, often depending on the student to have tuition at home to cope with their studies.

(Much like a baggage handler who, after 15 years on the job lugging heavy suitcases, shows no respect for, bashes about and rough-handles a lady's expensive Louis Vuitton baggage, which had probably been acquired by her spouse in a honeymoon mood.

The same could be said of some nurses in hospitals in a dead-end job. After the first few enthusiastic years, the smell of the hospital and the incessant demands of patients, the long hours and being constantly on their feet, does take a toll on their mental make-up.

What seems to be an emergency to a frantic family member of a patient becomes just routine to them, and sadly, that appears to the family members, and patients alike, as if the nurses are non-caring. Rightly so, in some cases, but, then, nobody wants to know the nurses drudgery.)

Moreover classes are not getting smaller, with more than 35 students in a class nowadays. Could be, it is the continuous pressure of having to complete a syllabus and the tendency to rush through a day's lesson that brings this about.
(What with all the marking to be done after school.)

And there is the partying, boozing and wooing, that is a natural part of life for most of us, since a lot of teachers are quite young, and expectedly, want to enjoy their lives.
(Bally did have a date with a teacher once, but she was so instructional, that he could not perform. He was definitely given an F! Her students the next morning must have got the brunt of her frustration!)

When Desiree was in primary 3, she was studying Malay as her 2nd language. Malay was not exactly a favourite of hers and having teachers like she had in her earlier 2 years in school did nothing to hold her attention or to interest her in that subject.

They had been really dull and uninspiring.

Her Malay Language teacher that year took the cake. She was the ultimate example of a teacher who had no idea of good teaching practices.

This teacher, Mrs. Kassim, would slither through the classroom door, puffing and wheezing after the one-storey climb to the class. How Desiree wished, in vain, that she would give one last gasp and collapse on the floor, never to rise again!

Dressed in a shapeless baju kurong, her head covered with a head-scarf, or selendang, she would look at the students through her owlish glasses with a stare that could melt 'ice-kachang' (a delicious Malaysian crushed-ice ball with sweet corn and red pea fillings, coloured with red and green syrup held in frozen sticky hands and sucked until the last icy drop!), a kilometer away!

She was by far the unhappiest looking teacher anyone had ever met and would likely meet. Middle-aged, grouchy, grumpy, gorilla-like, fat and ugly, together with an expression as if she chewed gum made of 'assam' (tamarind), she faced the class each day.

She just rattled off the day's lesson, reading from the text book, not pausing to explain anything.

There were no grammar or vocabulary pointers. Nor was there an explanation about the significance of the lesson. After 25 minutes of gobble-de-gook, to Desiree, at least, she wrote the day's assignment on the blackboard, left it there for about 3 minutes, and then wiped it off.

Some teacher!

All Desiree remembered, day after day, was her bulbous ass hiding the blackboard from her!
Then the teacher checked the previous day's homework of the students.

Of course Desiree had no idea what the homework was. She had had no clue what her teacher had been talking about. Nor did she have tuition for Malay.

Her elder sister, Sheryl, had her own problems with her 2nd language, so she was not much help at home. Both of them were also constantly quarrelling with each other; a case of sibling rivalry.

Mrs. Kassim always shouted at Desiree.
She used to call her *'Bodoh'* - meaning *'stupid'*.

Once she called Desiree to the front of the class, and

pulled her hair and twisted her arms, all the time cursing and swearing in Malay. The sadistic Che'gu thoroughly enjoyed herself, roughing her up. Desiree had no defense and tearfully submitted to the maltreatment.

She felt guilty at having done *'wrong'* for being hopeless in Malay. She felt unworthy. What right did she have to complain against the Malay teacher?

So what if the Che'gu badly ill treated her for purely academic matters at that?
At the same time, even in her muddled state of mind, she knew that the Teacher's actions were not right, but did not know what to do.

She continued to withdraw into her shell as her Malay got worse and worse and the injustice escalated.

Meanwhile she did not utter a word about the mistreatment to her parents. She did not go to them because she was always failing her Malay and not completing her homework and had been scolded for that already. Desiree never thought that they would understand that she did not comprehend the lessons and had no idea of what was required of her!

Instead it was the Che'gu who had reported her delinquent performance in class to her parents.

Her parents, though they knew she was having problems with Malay, did not pressurize her to study too hard for this subject. Her Father (that is ME!) was happy that she just pass. Eventually, though, he became apprehensive when she consistently failed this subject.

All this went on for some time, until one day, her Momma noticed some red marks on her upper arm. On inquiry, Desiree reluctantly told her that her Che'gu had pinched her arm and yanked on her hair because she had not done her homework.

Her Momma was very upset with her for not even attempting her homework, and as expected, initially did not understand the situation Desiree was in.

However, she was more distressed with the capital punishment handed out to her daughter by the teacher!

Ever seen a bear protecting her cub?
Well, Momma was in that mood when Desiree's Poppa came home.

He was told about what the teacher had done. His response was to scold a tearful Desiree, telling her that he had enough of her nonsense and that she deserved it.

Momma managed to persuade him to visit the Principal of the school and sort it out.

The next day, Poppa went to the school and met Mrs. Kassim in the Teachers' Room. His first reaction, on meeting her, was a question to himself - *"Is this teacher of the Human Species?"*

Foremost in Mrs. Kassim's mind was whether Desiree had tuition in Malay!

That was her cure-all. Then he was told that she was a very difficult and rebellious child who would not do her homework or pay attention in class.

Every chance to smear the hapless kid was attempted. All was fair game. Desiree was academically poor, her conduct atrocious, and motivation less than zero!

Poppa was shocked.
Was the teacher describing his sweet natured Princess or some strange creature of the wild?

He was determined to get to the bottom of the affair.
He managed to meet the Principal later.
Incredibly, the Principal echoed the Che'gu when she asked whether Desiree had tuition in Malay!

That served to strengthen his belief in the old adage, *"Great men think alike, Fools seldom differ."*
And it is applicable to both genders.

Poppa's hackles were raised; he had had enough.
He asked what the teachers were in school for.

Was it necessary for students to have tuition when there were fully qualified teachers in school?
(What was the point of students attending school in the first place?
Wouldn't it be better to just keep them at home and give them tuition in all the subjects until Exam time?
Parents would save on transport, uniforms, recess allowances, and, most importantly the time spent commuting!
After all, all that the future Employers looked for was just Paper Qualifications. So did it matter how the students obtained the requisite results?)

Why was that the first question both Mrs. Kassim and the Principal had asked?
Moreover, were teachers allowed to lay their hands on their pupils and mete out Capital Punishment?

Sensing that she had awoken a sleeping tiger, the Principal tried to diffuse the situation.

Poppa finally left the school with the impression that the Principal would talk to the teacher to at least explain the lesson of the day to the pupils. There was also an assurance that there would be no more physical action by the teacher.

(Little did he know that mental abuse is sometimes worse and how it would be meted out by the teacher on Desiree's fragile psyche.)

Desiree had been called into the office to tell her side of the affair and was witness to most of the dialogue between the 2 adults. She left the office in high spirits with Poppa and a joyful feeling that at least ADULTS were listening to her!

She went to school the following day floating on a blanket of clouds!

(Yes, it turned out to be black thunder clouds with embedded bolts of lightning!)

If, her teacher had approached her with compassion and changed her style of *teaching*, Desiree might have improved in her 2nd language. What really happened that day was the stuff little kids' nightmares are made of!

That morning, Mrs. Kassim puffed, panted and oozed into the class. She stood for a full minute at the front of the class, huffing, and nasally honking, while spitting nails through her muddy eyes.

She opened and closed her slit of a mouth, like a catfish out of water. She snorted deep and loud.
Maybe she even farted.

The children knew she wanted to say something.
They knew she was angry.

Her face had puffed up like a salamander's and was mottled deep purple red-black in colour. Her head moved around her massive neck with short sharp jerky movements like a manic, ugly, obese turkey.

Then her eyes settled and focused on Desiree.

Desiree thought she was going to die.
Her teacher's glare was solid. It was like a laser cutting into her flesh. Mrs. Kassim's eyeballs dug deep into her!

With a final thoracic spasm, Mrs. Kassim began speaking, if you can call it that.

She told the class that there was a pupil in the class who had been very naughty and was trying to cause trouble for her in school!

Not only that, the parents of that pupil had also tried their best to make her look bad. She said that they were *'kurang ajar'* (not educated).

Desiree was petrified. Poppa had been quite sure that the Principal would council the teacher.

But here was Mrs. Kassim throwing daggers and machetes at her with her eyes and body language, and though she did not name Desiree, it was quite obvious to the rest of the class who she was talking about!

She went on and on, in her high pitched, ambulance-siren nasal whine. Then she said that if she had a knife she would not hesitate to use it on the hearts of the whole family!

She would also provide a shroud and wrap the pupil in it. (Those familiar with a Muslim funeral would realize what this means; the dead body is wrapped up in a white shroud before burial.)

Most of this was said in broken English! Obviously she was conscious of the fact that if she had addressed the pupils in Malay, many in the class, especially Desiree, would not have understood her! Desiree went home sobbing that day. Her parents noticed her red eyes and inquired what was wrong. She had to tell them delete what Mrs. Kassim threatened.

You should have seen Momma hit the roof! The next day, Momma went to see the Principal, who was defensive and not very receptive to her. She tried to convince Momma that Desiree had probably made it all up.

Fed up with all this, Momma wrote to the Ministry of Education. A full investigation was carried out by the Ministry. Mrs. Kassim was eventually transferred. We never cared to find out where she went.
But it was too late in the year for a new teacher to salvage the class.

There was a 78% failure in Desiree's class in the Malay language that year. Needless to say, she was one of those that failed!

"That must have been a really obnoxious human being," Dino ventured.

"Human Being? That was no human being! She was an obese Monster!" Desiree screamed from her corner.

"Well, all of you kids think that teachers are ogres, don't you?" Kip asked quietly. *"Let me tell you about an*

occasion when students became real beasts."

"I bet that all of you had at one time or another fantasized the worst kind of torture and death for some teachers during your school years. I know I have been guilty of harbouring such fantasies about certain of my teachers, imagining the most horrible accidents and torture and death. Those teachers have been run over by steam rollers, hit by trains, blown up by atom bombs, set on fire by the kitchen stove, and even gored to final brutal death by the horns of bulls! And many other terrible endings. My imagination really ran riot sometimes!" Kip continued.

By this time most of the children and adults were nodding their heads, as you are doing, agreeing that he was correct.

"Hah! I knew it. But how many of you have actually achieved your fantasies? I would say that none of you have! Most of you students won't dare, mainly for fear of the consequences that would follow such an act. Plus, the authority and power wielded by the teachers do not encourage any such actions," he declared.

"However, a group of students in my class fulfilled its fantasy beyond its wildest dreams!"

CHAPTER 13

GOAL KICKS

Mr. Harnam was Kip's Math's teacher.

He was a good looking man. An athlete and a sportsman. He was a very nice person compared to some of the other teachers.

A gentle soft-spoken man most of the time, he would take the trouble to explain to us the math assignment before we went home to do our homework.

If he had a shortcoming, it was his mercurial temper. He became very upset with any students who did not complete their assignments.

As in every class all over the world, we had habitual laggards and these die-hards would not do the bit of work required of them.

Mr. Harnam tended to blow his top and get really angry and scold the pupils concerned. I think that he regarded himself as a very good teacher and any student not responding to him was taken as a personal insult.

Unfortunately for Mr. Harnam, we had a couple, in primary 4, of hard-headed boys who were not interested in school studies altogether.

These 2 were of a special breed!

They would sit at the back of the class and pass their day talking to each other or reading comics. Even though they were separated after the first 4 months, and made to sit in the front row, they still managed to avoid any due attention required of them during lessons.

The amazing thing was that these two, Kheng Hock and Kwok Hong, passed all their subjects with top results at every exam. Due to this, the teachers left them alone to their shenanigans in class and did not pressurize them.

Being a primary 4 class, word must have passed among the longer serving teachers that these two were an anomaly and were better off being left to their own peculiar ways!

Not so Mr. Harnam!

He could not accept the fact that a student of his who had been coached totally about his homework neglected the day's assignment. He was also relatively new to the school, being transferred there only the year before. As such, he was unaware about the peccadilloes of Kheng Hock and Kwok Hong.

So he raved and ranted at them almost every period. Of course they were immune to all his histrionics. After all, they had managed to educate and mould all their other teachers to their ways over the last three years!

Well, everybody has a limit. These two boys, not being able to wear Mr. Harnam down, were getting to dislike him intensely. He would not give up on them!

How did the two boys exact their revenge on Mr. Harnam? What made them turn into real beasts in such a short time? How did Mr. Harnam allow a pair of 10 year old kids to attack him physically? Why did 10 or 12 other normally well-adjusted children join these two in what occurred eventually?

Let me explain.

Dear soft-spoken Mr. Harnam had a problem.
He had a very serious problem.

Mr. Harnam was prone to fits.
He would suddenly turn stiff while talking to us in class. This happened at least once a month. The first time it happened was half-way into our maths class in the first month we had ever met him.

He was writing on the blackboard when he stretched up, twisted, uttered *"Ga! Ga! Ga!"* fell down on the floor and started thrashing around.

All of a sudden, he lay still.

We were terrified!

"Arrgghh, Arrrgghh," issued from his foaming open mouth. The whole class was shocked and it took one of us a few minutes to run next door to call the teacher from that class.

This teacher also went, *"Arrghh, Arghhh, Arrgh!"* when she saw his body on the floor. We thought she was going to join him on the concrete!

Eventually the Principal and half the canteen hawkers were in the class.
(Strangely, whenever something happens in school, the canteen people are always among the first to appear!)

An ambulance came and took him away.

We thought that that was the last we would see of him. Some of us were missing him already.

It was a hot topic in our homes that evening.

To our surprise, the next day, there was Mr. Harnam looking fit as a fiddle, standing before us for the maths lesson as if nothing out of the normal had happened the day before! He even scolded the two delinquents for not completing their homework!

Mr. Harnam had his next fit about 3 weeks later.
By now he had explained to the Principal about his condition and there was not much fuss this time.

Over the next 3 months we were entertained by poor Mr. Harnam's antics. During our break, we parodied his seizures and many of us would roll about the grass, going *"Arrgggghhh!! Arrghh! Arghhh!"* , tongue hanging out of our mouths with much eye-rolling.

One can only imagine what Kheng Hock and Kwok Hong were thinking at this time. The consensus later was that these two must have realized a golden chance sometime during those 4 months.

(Since they spent all their free time together, in school and on the outside, they must have had plenty of time hatching all kinds of plots.)

As for myself, I do not think that the terrible duo consciously crossed the barrier between respect for authority and the act of blatant physical assault on their teacher.

Most probably it was spontaneous.

It happened that in the middle of shouting at Kheng Hock, Mr. Harnam had one of his fits and fell down on the floor.

Kwok Hong is the one who calmly got up from his seat, walked up to the prostrate, helpless teacher and kicked him on the side of his chest.

I still remember the sound of that kick!
It was, *"Thwock!"*

We were all stunned.

Next, without a word, Kheng Hock went up to him, lifted his head as far as it could go and slammed it to the floor.

The teacher's head hit the ground with a loud thump. The two boys then coolly sat in their chairs until another teacher was summoned to attend to Mr. Harnam.

The rest of us were fearful.
That night at home, I could not sleep.
Nor, I believe, did all of the other pupils in that class,
except probably for those two devils!

Lo and behold, the day after, Mr. Harnam was in front of
the class with only a plaster on his forehead, patient as
ever and eager to continue his lessons. He seemed to
have no recall of any mistreatment whatsoever.

Whatever it was, those two rogues now knew for a
certainty that when their teacher had a fit, he did not
remember anything.

Things took a turn for the worst the next time Mr.
Harnam went down like a falling sack of potatoes.

Kheng Hock and Kwok Hong kicked their goals in using
his twitching body as a football, roaring gooaalll!
What happened next was astounding!

One timid Sikh girl, Meetha, usually very quiet in class,
went up and lightly tapped his head with her foot and
shouted, *"Goal!"*

That seemed to unleash something primeval in some of
the other kids in class.

One by one, some lightly and timidly, some with real gusto, they booted the body of their fallen teacher and serenely walked back to their desks!

Nobody now said a word.
After a few minutes, one of us raised the alarm that Mr. Harnam was having another fit.
He was tended to routinely and taken away.

Mr. Harnam obviously checked his body when he reached home and found a few bruises where none should have been!
And he did realize something was wrong because parts of his body hurt, particularly his back and chest, which he kept rubbing with a puzzled expression on his face.

The following day, he did not smile and greet the class as he usually did. He had an apprehensive look on his as yet, handsome, but drawn face. He definitely suspected something had happened but did not want to believe it.

Over the rest of the month, he became progressively quieter, and seemed to shrink into himself. He must have dreaded his next attack.

The class was also at its best behaviour. Most of us who had had no part to play in the beating were feeling terrible. We did not want to snitch on our classmates and tell him what had happened. We thought the best course was not to say anything.

Like Mr. Harnam, I was not looking forward to seeing him collapse again.

Which was what he did only 2 weeks later, far faster than at any other time. Perhaps his anxiety over this had precipitated an early spasm.

He gasped and fell down. This time, the expression on his face was even more desperate. He realized that the time had come and he was powerless to do anything about it. He lay down unconscious, twitching, uttering those weird noises.

There was no hesitation by those two misfits!

They ran up to his prone body and gleefully kicked him on his back and legs. One by one, 10 to 12 kids had a field day punishing him all over, before sedately returning to their desks.

Then Kheng Hock walked back to Mr. Harnam, bent down, reached into his pockets and pulled out some money!

We were all shocked! This was a crime indeed!

We could see that our teacher was in real pain when he recovered. He stumbled to his feet, grimaced, took a hasty frightened look around the class and was helped to the Teacher's Room by another teacher.

We did not see him for the rest of the day. The Principal came and tried to find out what had happened. Of course, none of us dared to tell him anything. Even when he became angry and resorted to threats of punishment against the whole class, he could not get anything out of us.

A new teacher was assigned to us for maths. We saw Mr. Harnam around the school for a few days after that, slinking around with drooping shoulders and a haunted expression on his now hollow-cheeked gaunt face.

We learnt that he was eventually transferred to another school. None of the culprits was caught.

The students in that class seemed to mature overnight. Kwok Hong and Kheng Hock were more attentive in class. They seemed to have got a bug out of their systems by the bashing of Mr. Harnam! Maybe the football sessions with their teacher had short-circuited the student's brains or maybe deep inside their heads they realized what kinds of animals they could turn out to be in the right (or wrong) circumstances and wanted to forget about it all. Kheng Hock and Kwok Hong shaped up their act and started to hand in their work regularly!

Kheng Hock is now a doctor while Kwok Hong is a district judge. I only hope that when he passes judgement on the accused before him, Kwok Hong remembers the violence and relish with which he attacked his defenseless teacher!

At this, Kip paused and took a deep breath. This was truly a long speech for him!

"Yes, It is too bad that the drugs that could keep his condition in check were still not on the market." Tara, who is a Doctor, noted.

"Poor Mr. Harnam, especially when you say that he was such a dedicated and kind teacher. He must have been traumatized by that treatment," commented Kulli.

"I too had a teacher once who was well liked by all the students in my school, but her story is much sadder."

"Tell us about her, please," Sheryl begged.

CHAPTER 14

TRAGEDY

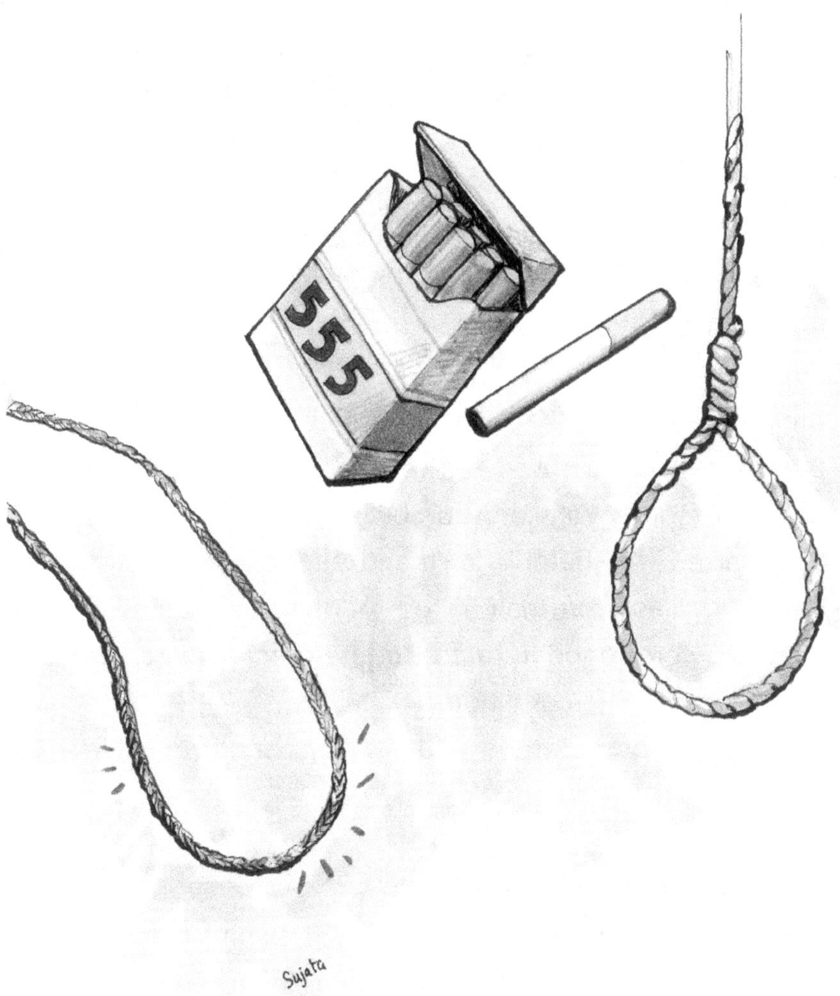

"Nalini was my history teacher," Kulli began.

A slim, small boned girl of 19 years; she was the daughter of impoverished labourers. She was the pride and joy of a community of rubber tappers in a plantation just out of Kota Tinggi where we were studying in Laksamana School.

No one else had managed to break out of the poverty trap and miserable life led by the rubber tappers and their families.

Brought in from South India to work in the rubber estates, they were paid a few cents a day for back-breaking work, in stormy rain or scorching sun, for a full day that started well before dawn and ended after sunset. Entire families, from half-naked toddlers to shambling old folks were roped in to collect the precious latex, in the most primitive conditions.
(While the Rubber Barons made millions and lived a life of luxury.)

Theirs was a truly a miserable lot.
Her success had given hope to all of them. She was supplementing her parent's income, to pay for the education of her two younger brothers who were coping very well at school, especially under her personal tutorage.

A few dollars went into her personal savings for her future.

This school also had children from other rubber plantations around the district where the parents had been encouraged by Nalini's status as a respected teacher and hoped that their children could be as successful!

Though most of the children went barefoot to school and seldom had money to buy books, they had enthusiasm and a very cheery attitude.

All of them from Nalini's little compound trooped behind her after school to board the same bus to the outskirts of town and then walk about a kilometer to their homes, along a dimly lit path.

Nalini was an extremely well-liked teacher.
I do not recall her being angry and upset or shouting at any student. She had a strange effect on the most unruly kids, who were usually rude to other teachers. But when Nalini walked into our class, there was an instant hush and everybody sat up straight.
It was as though she had cast a spell on them.

There was an inexplicable aura about her.

Occasionally, Nalini attended short meetings after school and the estate kids went back home without her. Then Nalini took the bus by herself and walked the desolate road home from the bus stop, often reaching her parent's quarters well after dark.

It must have been quite scary to do that!

One fateful evening, Nalini stayed back for a teachers' meeting. She then took the bus, dropped off at the bus stop and that was the last anyone saw her that night.

Her parents were worried when she did not reach home by 8 o'clock. Normally she would be at home at the latest 15 minutes after 7pm.

She had no known boyfriends and almost never went out at night. Her social life was with her beloved family, when once a month she would treat them to a trip to town to see a Bollywood movie and have dinner at their favourite dosa (a delicious South Indian thin oversized pancake-like dish made out of rice flour and served with curry and coconut sambal) stall.

At 8.30 pm, her parents were frantic. Her father took his ancient rickety bicycle and went along that lonely path with a handheld flashlight, forlornly calling out her name.

"NALINI! NALINI!! NAALINNIIII!!!"

All in vain.

When he returned home around an hour later after the batteries of his torch died, he went to the estate Manager's house and asked for his advice and help.

The Manager knew and liked Nalini. His son was also in my school and had obtained an *"A"* in History. He called the school and on receiving no reply - not surprising at that time of night - informed the police.

The police made a search of the path and the surrounding area.
It was dark and with no proper lighting, the search was unsuccessful.

That night the whole of the community gathered around Nalini's house. There was an intense feeling of dread and Nalini's father had tears in his eyes throughout the vigil. Her Mother was already wailing that she had lost her daughter and was inconsolable.

By a Father's sense, he knew that he would never see Nalini alive again; though he prayed to his Gods that nothing evil had befallen his Dear Angel.

A tiger attack was the foremost thing in his mind because a tapper had been killed and eaten just a month past in a plantation in the neighboring state.
The search was continued at first light.

Nalini was found about 200 meters from the bus stop, and 100 meters into the plantation from the path.

She had been strangled and suffocated by her head being pressed into the earth. Her mouth was full of dirt and there were blades of grass and soil in her lungs, indicating a horrible death.

She was still dressed in her sari, though the loose end had been looped around her neck to viciously strangle her.
Her gold chain and watch; the only ornaments she wore, were missing. Her purse, containing a few dollars and coins, a handkerchief and keys and a little-used lipstick had disappeared.

Nalini's parents were devastated.
What kind of Devil would harm their darling little girl?

The whole village was stricken with deep grief.
The only bright spark in their drudging existence had been savagely extinguished.

They never recovered from this tragedy.

A miserable gloom settled in that village from then on for a long, long time.

Even the subsequent success of her brothers and the other children in their education and careers did little to lift their spirits.

(These children were at that time still in primary school anyway, and the completion of their education was still far away in the future.)

What hit their hearts further was that matchmakers from all over the state had been visiting her parents for a suitable match for Nalini.

The parents and a blushing Nalini had already short-listed two likely virile candidates with civil service jobs.

When the news hit the school that day, we, students and teachers alike, could not imagine our much beloved Nalini murdered. We could just not picture her dead.

A few of the girls became hysterical.

The Teachers' Room was full of sobbing teachers.

The children who had attended her classes obtained ready permission to visit her home at the plantation and went there by bus.

Nalini's murder enquiry ended up in Father's lap.

He started his investigation at once. Within 4 days, Father had traced the gold chain to a pawnshop in Skudai, a small town not far from Kota Tinggi.

The chain had been pawned by a small-time crook, Osman, who had been in and out of jail many times before.

Father realized who he was immediately, since he had been responsible for apprehending Osman after his last comparatively petty crime, burglary, for which he had been sentenced for 13 months.

Osman had been released from prison just 2 months before Nalini had been found murdered.

A state-wide search was launched for Osman.

For a man who had just brutally murdered an innocent, helpless and compassionate young woman barely out of her teens, in cold blood, and now had the death sentence hanging over his head, Osman was amazingly careless about covering his tracks.

He had left his particulars in the pawn shop. He did not go into hiding. He was found the next day in his mother's house, playing cards with his neighbours.

He attempted a feeble struggle to resist arrest, but after that he was quite docile and was brought to the police lock-up without any problems.

Being a regular inmate of jail, he knew that if he did not resist strongly, the arresting officers had no reason to reciprocate with force too!

With all the evidence before him, Osman confessed to the killing.

Osman had seen Nalini on the bus previously, since he took the same bus to his kampong (village) a few kilometers down from the plantation bus stop.

He knew where she got off. And that the path to her home was feebly lit, with a streetlight every 200 meters. A lot of bulbs had blown out and not been replaced and certain sections were totally dark, especially on moonless nights and during the rainy season.

And he had noticed her gold chain and watch. His evil mind registered all this, storing the information until it was needed.

Unfortunately for Nalini, the need for him to use this knowledge came not too long later.

All that this callous killer had needed was money to buy his cigarettes.

Nalini's necklace, a thin gold chain worth not more than 40 dollars was going to enable him to buy a few packs!

In Malaysia, in those days, and I believe even now, there were no regular bus stops along a main trunk road linking small settlements.

All the passengers had to do was to ring the bell when the bus reached their destination. The bus stopped along the road, the passengers got off and the bus moved on.

Osman was familiar with this.

He was on the bus when Nalini boarded it outside the school that sad evening. He had not pre-planned to attack her.

That day, he just had a simple need to get some nicotine in his system. When he saw Nalini, his eyes fell on her chain and his mind went into overdrive.

Instantly, he knew what to do.

For a person who was eventually arrested for his sheer stupidity, he must have thought very rapidly and singularly that evening!

When Nalini alighted from the bus, he remained on board. 2oo meters down the road, he rang the bell and got down from the creaky bus.

As soon as the bus moved off, he ran back to the path leading to her settlement.

He overtook Nalini and attacked her, overpowering that poor little girl as she was walking down that gloomy path.

She was dragged into the trees. Despite her size, she put up a fierce struggle.
Osman wrapped the sari around her neck and throttled her. He pushed her face into the earth and beat her around her head.
With her face pressed into the ground, Nalini, in her desperate attempts to get some air into her lungs, breathed in and swallowed the grass and muck.
Nalini choked and stopped her struggles within a short time.

Osman removed her watch, chain, and purse and left the gruesome scene.

The watch was recovered from a neighbour of his, being given to him as a settlement of a previous debt. The purse was never recovered.

The chain was pawned in Skudai for 25 dollars. Enough to keep Osman in cigarettes for the next few weeks. Being the children of the chief honcho in town, we kids were given free access to the police station.

Tara and I went to the lock-up to see this monster. I will never forget his face. He looked up at us with empty eyes. Sitting on his bare cot, his hardened eyes did not have any expression.

Just a deep black bottomless evil!

I felt such a feeling of dread that I quickly went out of the police station into the sunshine.

Tara was not far behind!

Osman was hanged for his hideous crime.

For the need of a pack of cigarettes and a spikeful of nicotine, a whole happy, hopeful community had been stripped of all hope, laughter and spirit.

"Yes," said Kulli, sadly, *"It is terrible what happened to her. Such an innocent person did not deserve that kind of death."*

"Nobody deserves that kind of death!" Sheryl shouted out. *"I am glad that Grandpoppa caught Osman!"*
At this retort from Sheryl, Father, who had been reclining in his chair with his eyes closed, slowly opened one eye and acknowledged the looks of admiration on his grandchildren's faces.

He must have got thirsty again and I could see that he was scanning the crowd to see who he could send for another beer for him!

"There are other teachers I remember who were absolute terrors. One of them was Mr. Woon, your Art Teacher, Sam," Tara volunteered.

TURTLE TEACHER

Mr. Woon was a scrawny man of medium height. He had a long neck, dry wrinkled face and a short pudgy nose. His narrow head was covered with oily, thinning spiky hair, probably saturated with Tancho.

Rumour had it that his father had taken one look at him when he was born and never came back home!
He also had a habit of skewing his sharp head to the side when he was listening to someone.

Mr. Woon had, like most teachers, his favourites in the class. With these pupils, he was patient, often spending a long time at their desks, cooing and praising their work. He even took their pencils, crayons or paint brushes and helped them improve their work.

However, with a few of us, in his class, he could be, and was, a veritable devil. He often whined and moaned at us in a high pitched fluty voice. Nothing we did could be right. He was a real bitch with those unfortunates who could not draw.

What did I know of art?

If I am asked to sketch a house, all I can do is draw 4 straight connecting lines and put in 2 windows, a door and the roof with a chimney, so the end product looks like a yawning, lop-sided sleepy square with a hat!

He especially picked on Seng Poh, a quiet well-behaved boy, who as the months went by, hated the sight of him more and more.

This pent-up resentment came to a head one day when Mr. Woon asked the class to draw a picture of any object they saw in class.

He went around the class, passing comments.
Of course, when he came to his pets, he was all full of praise.

Slowly he meandered about the class and came to Seng Poh's desk, looked over his shoulder and recoiled.

His mouth dropped open and with head twisted to one side, he yapped, *"What is this? What stupid thing have you drawn?"*

Seng Poh replied calmly, *"A turtle, Sir"*

Mr. Woon asked, *"A turtle? Where do you see a turtle in this class?"*

After a few seconds of silence from the class in which you could hear a mosquito burp, Seng Poh declared, *"That is you, Sir!"*
The class roared with laughter.

"Wham!"
None of us expected Mr. Woon's next action. It was like a pistol shot. He had slapped Seng Poh on the back of the head and dragged him out of his seat. Muttering darkly, he pulled Seng Poh to the Principal's office.

Seng Poh was punished. He received 4 strokes of the best from the Principal on his posterior and was made to sit outside the teachers' room for the rest of the day. (So much for encouraging students to think outside the box!)

There was one happy outcome, at least for Seng Poh. It was the last time Mr. Woon picked on him physically, though he did glare at him from time to time!

"Wow! This Seng Poh must have real guts!" exclaimed Tasha. *"I wouldn't even dare to think of doing something like that."*

"Oh yes, A few classmates were a bit weird in their own way," I said, *"Some of them had really disgusting habits."*

MR. FLICK

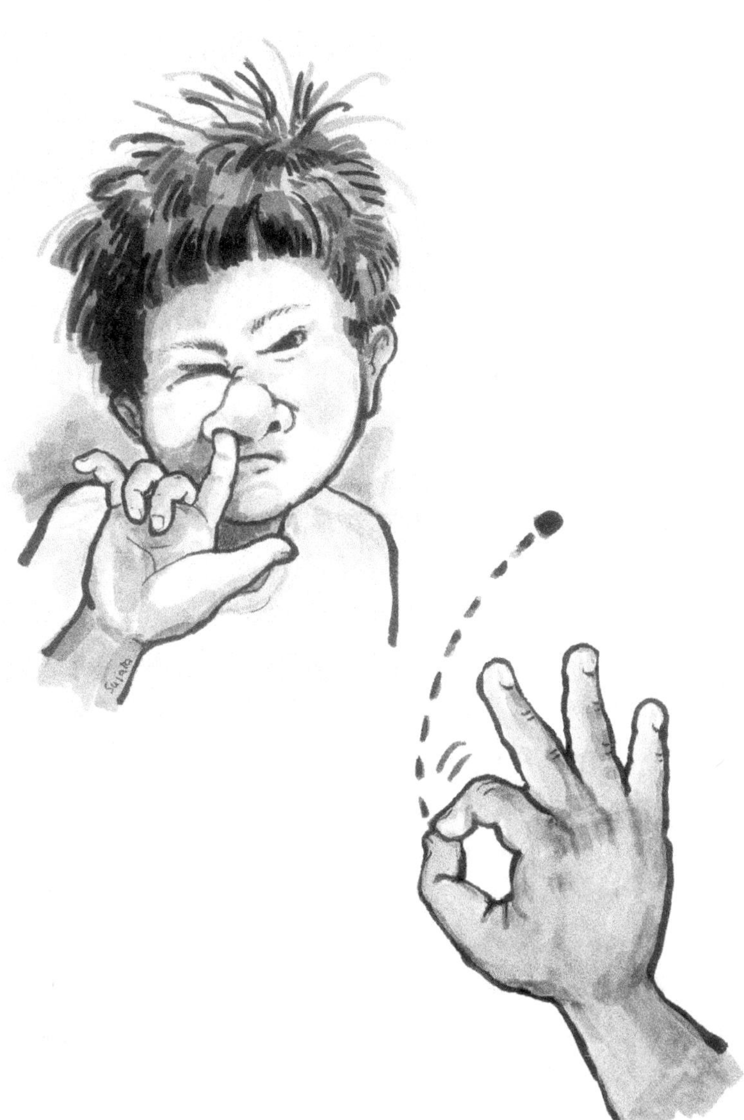

One of my mates in primary 5, Abu, was always chewing his fingernails. All his nails had been bitten to the flesh. Still he would go on, nibble, nibble, nibble.

He even gnawed on the soft flesh around his fingertips; so much so that they looked like raw lap-cheong (a Chinese red sausage often made out of dubious meat. Yes, elephant flesh has been used before!)
His parents even smeared garlic on his fingertips in an effort to deter him from gnawing his fingers to the bone!

This idiot apparently liked garlic, because that futile effort of his parents did not stop him!

There was another one, Anthony, also in primary 5, who was continuously scratching his head. Examination of his scalp revealed no evidence of lice or dandruff. Yet there he was everyday, scratch, scratch, scratch.

Other than the irritating sight of him scraping his head, his fingernails made a 'scritch, scritch' sound against his skull when he scratched. He also had a habit of carefully selecting a hair between two fingers, pulling it out of his scalp, and sucking on the hair root. His eyes closed when he did that!

Go figure!

If you think that was disgusting, let me tell you about Mr. Flick. He really took the cake.

Mr. Flick was so called because of his deadly aim with his nose boogers. His fingers were almost perpetually up his nose. He would dig and dig and dig, first one nostril, then the next.

How he managed to find a piece of nose *gold* every time he stuck a finger up, was a wonder to us.
He had a very productive nose!

Mr. Flick had a habit of flicking the boogers that he dug out at the blackboard whenever the teacher's back was turned to the class.

The teachers were always puzzled by those gooey streaks left on the blackboard whenever they erased it. One or two of them even tried to remove the lumps with their fingernails and fingertips!
After that, they had a hard time removing the gunk from beneath their nails. If only they knew!

As the year progressed, the side of the blackboard closest to where he was sitting was all covered with a mixture of grey and brown streaks of chalk and nose *gold*.

The wall next to him had little lumps and ridges, where he wiped his fingers. Some were brown and some were black. Some deposits looked like little dried up tadpoles glued to the wall!

The underside of his desk was also a favourite place of his to smear the sticky products of his industrious schnoz!

Nobody dared to sit on either side of him, because he used fingers on both hands at the same time sometimes. Everyone was scared that he wiped off his fingers on their uniform!

Obviously, nobody asked to share his sweets or food with them.

And god forbid if you upset him.
He would dig his forefinger far back in his nose, withdraw a black sticky ugly mass, and, flick! That dirty lump would hit your eye! If you opened your mouth to shout, it was a good chance that that glob would hit your tonsils!
He was that good.

If he was really angry, he dug both index fingers up his nostrils and let you have a double barrel - flick, flick!

Then, there was a kid in my primary 2 whom we called *"left side, right side"*. Maniyan was a small Indian boy, who was naturally quite untidy looking. His uniform, though clean, was always in disarray, with his shirt half-in and half-out of his pants, which he was constantly pulling up.

For some reason, he always used his left hand to pull up his pants. First he pulled up the left side. Then, with a strange agile twist of his body, he stretched his left hand to the right of his pants, bent down a bit and pulled up that side of his pants, straightening up suddenly. His other arm stuck out at right angles to his body.

This action always resulted in the left side of his pants sliding down. Then he started all over again! Pull up left side, twist; pull up right side, then the left side…

It was fun watching him at assembly when we had to stand up to 10 minutes at a time. Many a-times, a teacher or two shouted at him to stand still. He would, but only for a short while, and when his pants started slipping, he started his gyrations again.

We had a new teacher who noticed Maniyam's harmonic motions and yelled at him to stand still.

Maniyam tried very hard! He stood motionless. It was too much of an effort for him!

A minute or two passed.

Maniyam started to look around in despair, his head turning this way and that wildly. His normally black face turned purple with the effort.

(If you watch old South Indian movies, you will notice that most of the actors' faces appear purple, due to the efforts of the make-up artists to make them look fair. But that is another story and could be dealt with later.)

We can imagine the terrible battle Maniam had with his nerves that were twitching and jumping and the prodigious effort it took not to move his arms or body. His face was contorted with the furious struggle taking place between his nerves and his brain.

Finally, his brain lost out to his tortured nervous system! Frantically, he hitched up the left side of his pants and started his usual twisting and turning, but at a faster pace than usual.

Cruel as it may seem, all the students and some of the teachers laughed out loud at this spectacle. We just couldn't help it! Even though we were used to his antics, this was like fast-forward action.

The new teacher was quite upset but he was restrained from taking punitive action against Maniyam by Mr. Hong, our form teacher, who knew only too well that Maniyam was not doing it on purpose.

It was Mr. Hong who came up with a brilliant solution to Maniyam's problem.

He simply produced an old belt that had belonged to his son and shortened it to fit Maniyam's slight waist and presented it to him.

From that day onwards, Maniyam reduced his peculiar habit. He dropped it entirely after a few weeks.
He actually became a very studious pupil.

All thanks to an understanding and kind teacher who took the trouble and patience to identify Maniyam's problem.

"I must tell you about a few of MY classmates. They were really weird!" Sheryl cried out.

"I believe that a child's behaviour in class reflects the attitude and upbringing at home and the relationship of the child with the rest of the family, don't you agree?"

"Maniyam must have had problems at home to behave like he did. If Mr. Hong had not helped him, I think Maniyam would only have got worse." Ranjit, my brother-in-law observed. *"Anyway, Sheryl, what about your classmates?"*

"I especially remember Jessie and Gladys from my primary school days. They were surely strange cases." Sheryl related.

BROWN PANTS

We had this teacher in class, plump, ugly looking Mr. Lee. We called him Piggy behind his back.

One kid, Jessie, was absolutely terrified of him. Whenever Mr. Lee looked or even glanced at him, he started shivering. He did not respond to any query about his behaviour. He just sat and trembled.

As soon as Mr. Lee left the class, he became his normal self, laughing and joking with the rest of us.

His parents were eventually contacted by the teacher. His problem was revealed when his momma came to the school.

One look at Mr. Lee's face told her everything. She had to try very hard not to laugh out loud, though the problem with her kid was serious enough for Mr. Lee to call her in.

Her child had recurring nightmares. He always dreamt that he was chased by a fierce, wild, snorting pig boar with enormous tusks! And this wild pig was trying to gore Jessie to death and eat him up!

Jessie used to wake up screaming and shouting for his mother to save him.

After recovering from his nightmares, Jessie had to go to school and face Piggy in class.

Mr. Lee became the living, breathing wild boar of his dreams. Jessie's Mother was in a fix.

Can you imagine her telling Mr. Lee that he looked like a ferocious wild boar to her son? That he was a contributing factor to Jessie's shakes?

She, poor woman, finally picked up the courage to explain to Mr. Lee the problem. Surprisingly, Mr. Lee accepted her explanation without much distress. He must have had a lot of ribbing during his school days about his appearance and was quite probably resigned to accept the teasing! It was only when Jessie was persuaded to touch Mr. Lee, did his nightmares occur less often.

The reason why he had his tormenting dreams relating to Mr. Lee was never found. It was probably a weird coincidence!

After a few weeks, Jessie could often be seen talking to Mr. Lee with confidence. In fact, he became a sort of teacher's pet!

"So, that was Jessie. I also had this girl, Gladys, in my class in primary 1, whom I can never forget," Sheryl continued.

Gladys was a pale, shy girl.
She rarely uttered a word in class. Always neat and tidy, she spent her first few days in class silently sitting in her seat, without looking around, and her face buried in her books with her hair across her face acting like a curtain from the rest of the world.

(People, males as well as females, who let their hair hang down their faces so that it hides one eye, or both, when they are talking to you, always bother me. It appears that they are concealing something or guilty of something they don't want you to know. It also strongly suggests a feeling of inferiority! Anyway, that's my opinion, and if they want to hide themselves from the rest of the world or hide the rest of the world from themselves, whichever applies, that's their problem.)

It was on the fourth day of school, when Gladys suddenly started sobbing quietly.

Her teacher, Miss Gurmit, asked her what the matter was, but Gladys just shook her head and continued her muted crying.

She did not cry out loud.

It was more like a sniffling sort of sobs, just going on and on, monotonously, at a constant pitch and tone, *"hhhuuaahhhh, hhhuaaagghh, hhuaaahhh."*

Nothing Ms Gurmit said or did induced Gladys to voice out what was bothering her. After a while, the teacher left her alone.

Suddenly, Roger, who sat next to her, jumped up from his seat and stood there, holding his nose.

Miss Gurmit noticed him and asked, *"What is the matter with you?"*

All Roger uttered was, *"Smelly!"*

Miss Gurmit queried, *"What do you mean?"*
Roger snorted, *"Very smelly here."*

And he moved away from his desk still holding his nose, looking askance at Gladys. Miss Gurmit came up to their desk. As she drew up next to Gladys, she stopped dead in her tracks! Her hand came up to her nose, her eyes clamped shut and she just stood there for a few seconds.

She recovered, but still holding her nose, unintentionally gasped out, *"Gladys, what have you done? Have you shit in your pants?"*

Poor Gladys sank her head down on the desk and started howling. She would not look up, would not get up and would not shut up!

The teacher was at a loss at what to do next. She tried forcing Gladys out of her chair but Gladys had a death grip on the desk and would not let go.

Miss Gurmit then left the class to seek reinforcements and some advice.

While she was away, a few of the kids took the opportunity to mercilessly tease Gladys. Some children are very good at that! They have an innate tendency towards cruelty. They spot a weakness and God help the poor target!

Their actions only served to aggravate the situation and Gladys yowled louder than ever!

When Miss Gurmit returned with another teacher, the class was in a bedlam, some of the kids chanting, *"Shit-face! Shit-face! Gladys is a shit-face!"*

Add Gladys' bawling at the top of her voice and you can picture the bedlam.

The teachers shouted at everybody for silence.

Mercifully, the school bell rang at this moment for the end of the school day. Most of us were reluctant to leave since we wanted to see the fun, but Miss Gurmit chased us out.

It is a mystery to us how they cajoled Gladys out of her seat that day.

The next morning, Gladys was a few minutes late in coming to class, having missed her school bus and her parents booking a taxi for her, so the other students did not have the time to badger her before school started.

Thankfully for Gladys.

Her eyes were puffy and she looked miserable.

Miss Gurmit kept glancing at her apprehensively throughout her period. I think that she was worried that Gladys would repeat her performance of the previous day!

I also suspected that Gladys had not wanted to come to school and had been forced to do so by her parents.

However, the next week passed without incident, though Gladys was still mocked by some of her fellow students in class. She ignored them and retreated further into her curtain of hair and into her cocoon.

Then it happened again.

This time it was during a Maths lesson with Mr. Subra.

The same almost quiet sobbing, rising to open wailing when Mr. Subra tried to persuade her to get up. Roger jumped out of his seat like a rocket, holding his nose again and ran to the front of the class. Some of the other children followed suit, all pinching their noses and crying out, *"Gladys Shit! Shit! Shit!"* pointing at Gladys.

Mr. Subra was quite cool. Miss Gurmit must have briefed him about Gladys' problem. But being the good-hearted fellow that he was, he initially tried to reason with Gladys. That only raised the decibels of her caterwauling!

Faced with a crying, incomprehensible, uncommunicative member of the female species, he ran to fetch Miss Gurmit, who arrived breathlessly, whispered to Mr. Subra, said a few quiet words to Gladys and then left the class.

Gladys, to our surprise, suddenly ceased her bawling and behaved for the rest of the day.

Roger, of course, did not return to his seat and took the spare chair at the back of the class.

Gladys was left alone for the rest of the class period, which, luckily for her, had only about an hour to run. Once more we left the class with Gladys still sitting in her chair. As we left, we saw Miss Gurmit rushing to our class.

This happened twice more over the next few weeks. Each time it was near to the end of the school day and Miss Gurmit attended to Gladys. She was very patient with her.

She never raised her voice again, as she had on the first episode with Gladys. Perhaps she hoped that over time Gladys would snap out of the disgusting habit.

Well, Gladys did stop her crapping in class, but it would be many years before I found out the reasons she shat in her pants in class.

When I completed my primary session, I was transferred to a different school to start my secondary education.

I, as an ex-pupil, and an excellent runner, was invited to take part in an invitation relay whenever that primary school had its annual sports day.

It was there when I met Miss Gurmit again. We got to talking about old times and discussing previous school mates. I remembered Gladys and asked Miss Gurmit about her.

Ms Gurmit was quite willing to talk about her.
(Maybe it was because it had been one of her crowning successes with a difficult pupil. Understandingly, she was proud of it!)

What she told me that day opened my eyes as to how different other families could be, compared to my own.

Gladys came from a very odd family. She had two younger brothers. Together with their maid, there were 6 people residing in their well-appointed condo.

Her father, an advertising executive, had paranoia about cleanliness and hygiene.

Through one of life's many quirks, he had a wife who shared his idiosyncrasies.

In fact, in many ways, the wife was worse.
It was through her that the message of ultra-cleanliness was transmitted to the kids!

The family never visited a hawker centre - it was unhealthy, unhygienic and totally out of bounds!
God only knew what germs were lurking there looking for a ready pliable victim to invade and infect with vile diseases.

The one concession they made was to visit McDonalds, but only after intense scrutiny by the father, of the work area behind the counter.

Each child in that family had its own towel, own bar of soap, own blankets, pillow, forks and spoons, and given strict instructions not to use one another's belongings!

If you think this is unbelievable, each child and the maid were also given their own toilet rolls!
(The rational behind this escapes me, because, if you think about it, who would want to use a used toilet paper! And how would you even get hold of it if it had been flushed away?)

Moreover, God help them if they used that toilet roll too fast! They were forbidden to use any public toilets.

Even before they went to McDonalds or to visit their grandparents, the family had to line up at the 2 bathrooms at home so that they would not have a need to visit any public loos when they were out of the house!

Therein lay poor Gladys' problem.

From a very tender age she had been under instructions not to use any other toilets except the ones at home or those approved by the parents. Not having attended a day-care centre during her pre-school age, she was suddenly transported from her nice apartment to primary 1 at a public school! She diligently voided herself at home before leaving for school.

For her, the crap literally hit the fan when she had an urge to go to the crapper during her school hours!

Most times she could hold back until she reached home. Even during recess, she did not think of visiting the canteen or the washrooms. After all, her maid had packed her sandwiches for recess and that together with a small bottle of mineral water, was sufficient for her.

This explained why her problem only arose during the latter part of school hours.

That poor kid held on and on until she could not hold the rising turmoil in her intestines any longer. She probably never knew what a public toilet; much less a school toilet looked like! And she did not have her trusty personal roll of toilet paper.

Even if she was at the point of voiding her bowels, she did not have a clue of where to go or whom to inform that she was in dire need to visit the loo!

Her ever-careful parents had neglected to brief her about this likely event!

So Gladys sat in her seat and shat in her panties and let it all come out.

She was lucky to have a teacher like Miss Gurmit who suspected that something was physiologically wrong here and who was so understanding and patient with her.

(You would not like to imagine what would have happened if she had got a harridan like Desiree's Malay language teacher.)

After the first episode, Miss Gurmit, who cleaned her up, realized that something was amiss when Gladys insisted that she had to use her own toilet paper to clean herself. The big problem was that Gladys had no toilet paper on her! Moreover, plain toilet paper would not have helped her in that situation at all! What she needed was a wash with plenty of flowing water, and a change of clothes.

When Miss Gurmit finally managed to coax her out her seat and took her to the school toilet, Gladys resisted strongly and refused to enter. Only after gentle persuasion by her teacher did Gladys allow herself to be washed and dressed in a pair of school PE shorts.

Of course the pupils she was sharing the school bus with had to wait for her for a while. When she boarded the bus in her shorts and a plastic bag in her hands, she was mercilessly taunted.

She obviously got hell from her maid when she reached home that first day. That is probably why she looked so terrible the next day she went to school, having resisted dressing up and finally needing a taxi to get to school.

Perhaps it was not so strange that her parents did not approach the school until the third time that Gladys soiled her clothes and went home in PE shorts.

The maid must have been horrified when Gladys came home dressed like that, carrying an aromatic plastic bag with her undies and skirt, despite Miss Gurmit's efforts to rinse them! All her efforts to elicit an explanation from Gladys had been met with a wall of silence.

To protect her job, the maid finally informed Gladys' parents after the third time. After all, both of her parents were at work until the evening and the maid was in charge until they returned.

When they called the Principal's office, they were very aggressive and demanded to know what the school had been doing with their precious child!

The Principal invited them to visit her in the office to discuss the situation.

She consulted Miss Gurmit who briefed her on the child's problem and her suspicions about the situation in her home, having probed Gladys gently.
When they marched into the office, they were very defensive, blaming the teachers for their daughter's situation.

They even threatened to pull Gladys out from the school! The Principal was very patient with them but they left in a huff, warning the teacher to be more careful with their daughter.

As Miss Gurmit had managed to get the confidence of Gladys, she gradually learned of the family's peccadilloes.

The next time that the parents confronted the Principal was also the last time that Gladys poo-pooed in class. The Principal was sure of her facts and had the ammunition to reply to their accusations about the school and the teachers.

The parents finally sheepishly agreed that they might have been at fault in the first place. They promised that they would tell Gladys to use the school toilet as and when she needed to.
Miss Gurmit drove the nail in deeper when she pointed out that if a child is protected too much from dirt or denied access from the more common bugs, the child does not build up a resistance to them!
The kid is therefore more prone to the tiniest corkscrewed wicked bug that manages to find itself into that fragile body!

Despite the assurances from her parents, it took the teacher some effort to coax Gladys to use the toilet freely.

A lifetime of habits and instructions were very hard to break!

The crux came when Gladys was in urgent need to go a few days later and Miss Gurmit was luckily the teacher in class.

Gladys meekly raised up her hand.
Miss Gurmit, immediately, since she had been waiting for just this moment, led her to the toilet and left her alone to tend to herself.

From that day on, Gladys always waited for her, and her only, to request to leave the class due to pressing needs.

At first the teacher escorted her. Within a couple of months, Gladys was seen eating at the canteen, heartily digging into a bowl of mee rebus!

If Miss Gurmit had not handled this matter with the sensitivity and care she showed, I shudder to think what would have befallen Gladys and her younger brothers!

Sheryl, having completed her narrative, looked set to talk some more.

Bally, who asked rather mischievously, *"Does that explain why your Poppa raided his piggy bank one day?"* interrupted her.

At this, everybody looked at me in expectation.

"Shut up! Let Sheryl tell us more about her classmates!" I shouted, desperately trying to shift attention back to her. It was not to be so. They were lusting for blood and demanded that my story be told first.

Maybe they found my stories to be more interesting! Well, I could give as good as I got at this stage of my life. If they were so desperate to hear about that, I would oblige, if only to prove that what Sheryl said about the family having an influence on a child's behaviour was, in part, correct!

SWEETS AND SOUR

"How much did you kids get for recess when you were in primary 1? I bet it was no less than 1 dollar! Some of your classmates got as much as 5 dollars. Am I right?" I asked the grand-kids gathered around.

There were nods of agreements from them.
Anita even declared that the amount was not enough!
Well, she should have been in my shoes.

When I was in Kindergarten, in Suleiman School in Bentong, I was given an F&N bottle filled with home-made rose syrup, closed with a cork, and a jam sandwich, neatly packed by Mother. Some mornings there would be a paratha with *'achar'* (pickles).

I do not know until today why I was so fixated on the canteen food, since Mother was about the best cook in the world! But as I say, the grass is always tastier when it is across the fence!

Maybe it was just the need to join my peers when they ate during the recess. Or perhaps I realized at an early age that money does buy friends! It was simple logic; if you had no money, you could not socialize! And if you could not do that, you had few friends.

How envious I was of my free-spending classmates who had 10 cents to spend!

At 5 cts for nasi lemak, (coconut rice with small fried fish, a piece of omelet and chilli paste) and 5 cts for a bottled drink, they were rich! How often the envy and the need to be like your peers leads to crime!

And to crime I turned.

I had a piggy bank - a cute little fat piggy made of china, with big round eyes and a short curly stiff tail, rose red and pink-white in colour. It had a slot on its rounded back, to drop the coins in.

Though I did not receive any money for recess, I did get a few cents now and then for chores done around the house, like washing the family car or gardening- or for no reason at all when my father was in a good mood; then he just dug in his pockets and threw them at me, especially when he had had a beer too many.

All that money would go into that fat little porcelain piggy, under my Momma's diligent eye, to be used to buy a present for birthdays or on Deepavali, when a dial on its belly would be unlocked by a simple key held by Mother and the coins gushed out in a torrent onto a towel.

The required amount for the gift would then be carefully counted out and the excess coins reinserted into the slot until the need to buy another item.

Now, this little rose red and pink-white piggy was looking more and more attractive each day!
And the heavier it got, the more alluring it became to a penniless soul like me.

That piggy was going to solve my financial problems at school! I was going to get my nasi lemak by hook or by crook.

After many days of doubt, guilt and fear, I finally gave way to crook and the hook!

One day, when Mother was in the kitchen, Father at work and the rest of the family at school, I scurried to my bedroom.

With trembling fingers and knees, ears alert for any sound from the kitchen, I gingerly lifted the piggy from its shelf. With the slot on its back and no key for the lock, I had to turn it upside down to get the coins out.

I did that over the bed.

The noise of the coins crashing against the sides of that fat little porker would have woken up the dead! Anyone who has heard a cement mixer at work should understand what I mean.

I felt my heart stop beating!
My blood pounded in my ears.

I held the piggy in the air for a terrible two minutes, not daring to move. My arms ached. I was dizzy and faint. Mercifully and surprisingly, even with her bionic ears, Mother did not hear anything.

I continued with extreme care.

I used one of my Mother's bent hairpins (the hook) and poked round in the slot. Arms a-trembling, nerves jumping at every clink the coins made, I sweated buckets, until, PLOCK! a coin dropped onto the bed sheet.

A twenty cent coin! A fortune!

Now I had the coin, an upside down piggy bank, exhausted arms and no idea how to get that awful, cute little fat rose red and pink-white pig upright again without sounding like an off-key Chinese funeral band!

I carefully held the swine up with my right hand. I inched out my left hand and managed to grab a corner of the blanket, raised it and wrapped the piggy in it. Then, slowly, degree by degree, I turned the fat monster around. The muted clinks and clashes the coins made in that round belly, were now barely audible.

At last the obese porky was standing in its rightful place on the shelf! I stood looking at it in victory, wet with sweat, quaking with the tremendously perilous effort I had made.

It stared back at me with those glassy round big pig orbs, as if to say, *"Oink! You haven't heard the last of this!"*

I turned my attention to the 20 cent piece lying on the bed. Have you ever tried to hide a 20 cent coin? Especially when you are guilty of a capital crime?

If you are innocent, you could carry a television set on your shoulders down Orchard road in Singapore in broad daylight, with full confidence, knowing that you have fully paid up for it and that it belongs to you legally.

But a 20 cent coin taken from the stomach of your piggy bank illegally?

It attains the size and weight of a bullock-cart wheel.
It is impossible to hide it.

I tried to put it in my pockets. That 20 ct coin felt like a loadstone. It was so heavy.

I was sure that if I walked out of the room with it in my pocket, Mother would not fail to notice it bulging out of my shorts- even those shorts I had that could accommodate an airliner!

I next tried my pencil box.
That was also too risky.
Mother might decide to check whether I had all my pencils, ruler and other stuff required for school.

I put the cursed coin in my shoe.
It felt like Mount Everest in there!

I finally found a flap deep inside my bag and hid the coin under It. What a relieve it was to leave my house for the walk to my school!

I sidled out the front door, and then broke into a run as soon as I reached the path down the hill. I threw my jam sandwich at Dara Singh as I ran past it and he gobbled it up in one sucking gulp.

I flew to school on winged feet.
You should have seen me that day at recess!

I was at the front of the queue for Nasi Lemak at the canteen! It was heavenly.

I think I beat Dara Singh wolfing down the sandwich, such was my need for that dish.
All of a sudden my nasi lemak was gone.

Finished.

I licked the last of the sambal chilli off my fingers and sighed. I then had that much longed-for bottle of carbonated drink.

I still had 10cts left!

Burping happily, I strutted up and down the canteen stalls. What a decision to make!

I finally bought an iced lolly.
With my last 5 cts, I got myself a packet of sweets.

That is when I met Kip, who had come into the canteen for his break. I ran up to him and innocently offered him the sweets.

He did not say a word. Nor did his fat oily face betray any emotion.

In fact he took most of the sweets and handed back an almost empty packet before going off with his friends.

What a court-martial awaited me at home after school!

That big oaf brother of mine, that Judas, had snaked on me!

He stood smirking in a corner when my cute little fat rose red and pink-white piggy was brought forward as evidence of my felony. There was no denying the scratches around the slot that had been produced by my frantic jiggling and poking around with Mother's twisted hairpin!

Needless to say, I got more than six of the best of the bamboo switch that evening!

But I will never forget that day!

The day I stood in front of the hawker in the school canteen and shouted, *"One Nasi Lemak!"*

And proudly paid cash for it.

"*Nasi Lemak is still one of your favourites to this day!
You can't seem to have enough of it,*" my wife, Jita
said.

"*Since you are talking about food, I will tell you of an
occasion when I made a real ass of myself,*" Banso
volunteered.

BAD MEAT

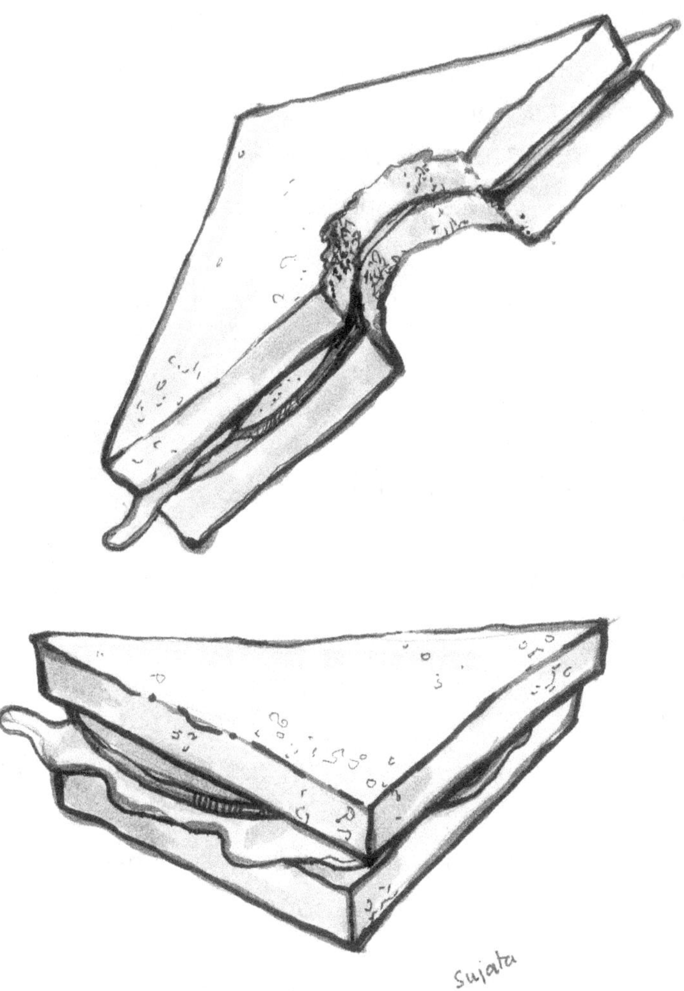

We sometimes unintentionally land ourselves into situations from which we find it hard to extricate ourselves.

"As you all know, Mother used to pack sandwiches for us to take to school most times," Banso started. *"Since she usually packed more than I could eat, I shared them with my good friends during our morning break."*

One day, I asked Aminah to share a sandwich with me. She enjoyed it and said it was very tasty.

When I went home that day, I told Mother that Aminah had really liked her cooking.

Mother was horrified. She told me that the sandwich contained ham!

Now, ham at that time came mostly from pigs.
(They have beef, turkey, and chicken ham nowadays.)

Aminah was a Muslim. Muslims don't eat pork!
Pork is not a *'halal'* (clean) food item for them. It is taboo.

We did not know what to do.
Should I tell Aminah that she had eaten pork?

What would she do?
Would I lose a very good friend?
What would her parents do?
What would the local Muslims do, when word got out about the matter?

This could lead to a major racial issue!

We tried to put ourselves in the same position. As Sikhs we did not eat beef. What if we had eaten beef without our knowledge? Were we committing a sin?

Mother and I decided to wait until Father came home from work. We presented the dilemma to him.

His sagely advice was to forget about the matter.

As I had innocently offered the food to Aminah and she had, also innocently eaten the forbidden ham, both of us were not to blame. Being honest with Aminah would only create a bigger problem!

One way I could satisfy my guilty conscience was to pray to my Nanak for forgiveness for being so thoughtless and to guide me to be more careful in future!

That is what I did.

I confess, I felt much better after that.

Moreover, from that day onwards, Mother was very cautious not to pack any more pork-related products into our recess packs!

As for Aminah, she did continue to share my food. And she loved every tasty bite of it!

As Banso finished her tale, Tara shot out at her. *"You claim to be a Sikh, yet I see you at McDonald's every other month, guzzling down the burgers! What are burgers made of?"*

"You silly fellow, if you took the trouble to notice, I always eat Fish Burghers!" Banso retaliated hotly.

As they were bickering among themselves, Peggy sent her daughter to fetch the last of the pizza and chips as it was getting late and everybody feeling a bit peckish.

Returning with the tray, she tripped over my outstretched legs and went sprawling, dropping the food on the patio floor.

"Look at what you have done!" Peggy screamed at me. *"Your whole life, you have been messing things up!"* (Forgetting about the foul gastric fountains she used to

spout in the car.)

There was a chorus of insults hurled at me from all sides.

"Whoa," I said, *"I have been lying here the whole night. She should have looked at where she was stepping."*

Sharon was sobbing by now, having injured her knee.

Her mother got up to attend to her. Father lurched to his feet, and proceeded indoors, to bed.

Mother started clearing up the mess, together with Beeba. The rest gathered up their kids, preparing to bed down, and the party broke up.

I was left to myself.

"Oh, no!" I muttered.

"Not again! I am being blamed for a quick end to the night!"

Soon, there I was, quite alone on the patio, gazing at Orion's Belt, wondering where I had gone wrong.

Of course, I knew that it was late and everybody was just looking for an excuse to call it a night.

What I could not understand was why it had to be because of me!

Again.

FALL GUY

The shock, the humiliation and the helplessness of being accused of and punished for something a child did not do has been experienced by almost every kid sometime or other during their childhood days.

There are also adults who seem to be prone to this and take the brunt of the blame of almost everything that goes wrong around them.

I seemed to be a natural choice for my fellow students and teachers to be a target of censure.
I was always in the wrong spot at the wrong time.
Sometimes I was the right guy in the wrong place!

It could have been my appearance acting as a magnet for trouble.

As a young kid, looking at photos of that period, I was a rather weird-looking boy.

Even now, as I look at those pictures, I want to accuse that pathetic, scrawny child in shorts too big for him, leering at the camera with teeth too big for his mouth, arms too long for his body, legs too thin for his huge feet, a head too big for his neck, ears too small for his face, for all the things that had gone wrong in my life!

One of my teachers, Mr. Soon, was a short, neat, compact person. He had a brisk way of walking and talking. His hands were constantly on the move, as were his eyes.

Except when they alighted on me.

Then he froze in that position, his eyes focused my eyes. As soon as he had contact with my eyes, he raised his eyebrows.

All this took only a fraction of a second.
In fact I don't think that any of the other pupils really noticed that. To me it was an eternity.
I cringed in my seat, trying to disappear.

I remember once, Alfred Wong was questioned by Mr. Soon as to why his homework was not passed up.

Now, Alfred Wong was a habitual non-passer of homework. Any teacher should have realized it by then.

He was always late in passing up his homework; that is if he had done it in the first place.

Sometimes he claimed that he had lost his book, at other times it was that he simply forgot to do his work.

Once he told his maths teacher that his grandmother had died the previous Friday and that he had had no time to complete his assigned work over the weekend. His teacher believed him. She even hugged and sympathized with him!

He was so successful that he repeated this same story with all the other teachers. His grandmother must have died at least 8 times that year! After all, he had 2 grandmothers to choose from, and he never did specify which one had died on any one day.

When this episode with Mr. Soon occurred, one of his grandmas had only died twice, so he had still not realized the full potential of a dead or dying grandmother and he did not exploit it to the full extent!

Then, when Mr. Soon questioned him on this particular occasion, he realized that he had already exhausted his repertoire of a lost book and other paltry excuses with this teacher.

Alfred Wong sat silent for a while.
He looked around the class and grinned sideways at me. He got up from his chair, pointed a finger at me and declared, *"He borrowed my book and didn't give it back"*.

What a lying bag of rice husks!

A-ha!
That must have been exactly what Mr. Soon had been waiting for!

All those previous weeks when I had sat timidly huddled in my chair when he was around, not daring to breathe, not moving, nor sneezing, nor coughing, barely blinking, I had never given him an excuse to pick on me.

He had bided his time!

Now, he spun towards me, his glasses nearly falling off. His scanty eyebrows shot up into his hairline, almost merging as one. He pointed his finger at me, face reddening, and uttered, *"You…, You…, You…!"*

He seemed incapable of saying anything else.
His finger continued pointing at me, quivering in the air, his hand and the arm it was attached to fully extended at shoulder level.

I think he was actually caught off-guard.

After weeks of staring at me - this scrawny, ugly specimen of humanity, who was obviously guilty of something, yet until now had been too smart for him to fault, despite all his vigilance - had finally screwed up!

The shock and the joy that his instincts about me had been proven correct had probably rendered him speechless.

After endless seconds, he recovered.
His expression changed. In orgiastic ecstasy, he smiled.

Oh, that smile turned my bowels into water. My stomach convulsed with cramps. I closed my eyes.

If Alfred Wong's accusation caught Mr. Soon by surprise, and rendered him orally handicapped, think of the effect it had on me!

All I could think of at that time was, *"Oh no! Not me again!"*

Though I was quite used of being accused and punished for crimes I did not commit (it was a way of life for me!), I was totally unprepared for Alfred's blatant false claim.
My mind went totally blank. My eyes saw nothing.

What happened after Mr. Soon smiled was as if I was in a hazy dream.

He raved, ranted, and pushed me around.
I started sobbing with fright and confusion.

We finally ended up in the Principal's office, where I received two strokes of the cane on my tender fleshless buns.

To add insult to injury, the other pupils laughed at me when I returned to class, Alfred being the loudest!

Word must have spread around because after that episode some of the other teachers would look at me queerly when they entered the classroom.

I became the fall guy, the patsy, to take the blame for any mischief created by my classmates.
(As I said, young children, though they may be slow in their studies, are very quick to be merciless!)

On another occasion, one of the kids threw a rubber at the blackboard when the teacher was writing on it.

I happened to reach down to pick up a pencil I had dropped and was fingered by the teacher as the culprit. Again I was hauled off to the office and given 2 of the supple biting rattan.

This time my parents were informed that I was a delinquent. Father, a strict disciplinarian, did not take kindly to this bit of serious information and my bony butt took more punishment, despite all my protestations!

Even at home I was not spared.

Once when my younger brother, Bally, and I were having a rough and tumble on the floor, he slipped by himself and fell flat on his face. He chipped a front tooth.

That kid set up such a-bawling and a-yodeling that Mother came rushing up. Taking a look at his bloody, bloodied mouth, she yanked me by my head, and blaming me for his mishap, administered capital punishment.

Even now, many years later, when we are having a whiskey or beer together, the subject comes up. But my brother still does not tell the truth about what occurred that afternoon, when he chipped his tooth. But in consolation, I must say that he went through most of his school life and early adulthood with a grin like a broken brown clay bed pan.

It was only when he started working that he could afford to patch up his Halloween smile with some cheap dental work and now he avoids smiling because if he did, his front false tooth looks like a shiny enamel coconut scraper.

And also, through the passage of time, and the way our personalities have evolved, I suspect Mother has realized that I was telling the truth after all. But even she does not admit she may have made a mistake.

Events like this have been part and parcel of my life. I accepted them because that was the way it was in those days.

You were supposed to grin and bear it .

I relaxed on the floor for some time, the rest of the family being busy with the bedding arrangements.

I could hear the children choosing who they wanted to be sleeping next to, with the Mothers and elder siblings putting in their two cents worth.

Suddenly, I heard Tasha and Hanz screaming at each other, quarrelling over the choice of sleeping positions.

I also heard Jita shouting at them, telling them to *"Behave, or else!"*

All was quiet. Or so I thought.

Suddenly there was a patter of running feet, and the front door blew open followed by a rush of bodies.

'What now?" I thought.

It was only my 4 kids, rushing out to be the first to say goodnight to me!

I was leapt upon and there was a flurry of kisses on my cheeks and a chorus of 'G'Night! G'Night! Love you!"

Before I could recover, they were on their way to their rooms.

It was nice.

I smiled and finished the dregs of my beer.

It was comforting to know that nothing had really changed since I was a kid.

Quarrelling, fighting, bullying, favouritism, jealousy, insecurity, were all part of growing up.

But the most important element, LOVE, among the family was always the binding factor.

If any of the tribe got in trouble, the world had better watch out!

Thanks, Reader for sharing my life at a young age.

I survived the many tribulations.

It could be because I did not know any better.

There are many instances when it is said that certain asides may be addressed later.

Please don't look for them as there aren't any!

Just look out for my next book which is going to be explosive!!

Until we meet again, I will put pencil to paper!

Sarmukh
e-mail: deskbrain2002@yahoo.com